Get an Inner Life
MEDITATE

Freedom is Found Within
Two men behind prison bars… One saw mud…the other saw stars!

Doreena Durbin

BALBOA.PRESS
A DIVISION OF HAY HOUSE

Balboa Press books may be ordered through booksellers or by contacting:

Balboa Press
A Division of Hay House
1663 Liberty Drive
Bloomington, IN 47403
www.balboapress.com
844-682-1282

Because of the dynamic nature of the Internet, any web addresses or
links contained in this book may have changed since publication and may
no longer be valid. The views expressed in this work are solely those
of the author and do not necessarily reflect the views of the publisher,
and the publisher hereby disclaims any responsibility for them.

The author of this book does not dispense medical advice or prescribe the
use of any technique as a form of treatment for physical, emotional, or medical
problems without the advice of a physician, either directly or indirectly. The
intent of the author is only to offer information of a general nature to help you
in your quest for emotional and spiritual well-being. In the event you use any
of the information in this book for yourself, which is your constitutional right,
the author and the publisher assume no responsibility for your actions.

Any people depicted in stock imagery provided by Getty Images are
models, and such images are being used for illustrative purposes only.
Certain stock imagery © Getty Images.

Print information available on the last page.

ISBN: 979-8-7652-5491-2 (sc)
ISBN: 979-8-7652-5490-5 (e)

Library of Congress Control Number: 2024917298

Balboa Press rev. date: 11/05/2024

DEDICATIONS

I dedicate this book to my adult children, Tamara and Derek as they were the driving force behind my striving to become who I am today. Taking on the responsibility of raising them with unconditional love, I allowed them to follow their dreams. They were set on a path to become independent and free to be whoever or whatever they wanted to be. They learned how to connect with their inner beings and create a better life for themselves and their families. Offering a little motherly advice from time to time, a warm hug, and a shoulder to cry on when life got tough, went a long way to prepare them for future challenges. They learned that with motivation and discipline, challenges can be overcome. Not everyone was born into a life of privilege so teaching them how to overcome challenges while accepting what they cannot change can make reaching success sweeter and more rewarding.

My son and daughter each had a son so I have been blessed with two cherished grandsons. They are the loves of my life. I hope that the boys will find their source of peace and happiness in the challenging world. With the expansion of social media, humanity is fraught with challenges. My hope is for the boys to follow their passions using their inner knowingness and intuition to choose a life path and career that resonates with their Beings.

I also dedicate this book to the incarcerated inmates who are caught up in penal systems around the world. They have been instrumental in helping me become a better more compassionate teacher as I listened to their stories and offered hope and healing. My deepest desire is for the inmates to realize that their misdeeds do not define them and they have the power to change their lives as they connect with their inner spirits. They can be a source of good by continuing on their spiritual journeys and making contributions to society, in positive ways by carrying the teachings forward to help others learn the power of meditation, new thoughts, and life skills.

CONTENTS

CHAPTER 1
INTRODUCTION

I walked into the men's prison, which is surrounded by razor wire fences, to teach prisoners my first "Get An Inner Life: Meditate" class. Several metal gates slam behind me while curious inmates follow me with their eyes. Being the only female in the courtyard, I am an anomaly standing at 4'11". As an empath and intuitive, I am acutely aware that the energies in the prison environment are rife with fear, anger, and despair. There is tension in the air. I hear a prison guard shouting at an inmate and witness him being detained with handcuffs. I trust that the Universe has my back as I breathe in pure positive energy. I energetically surround myself with an invisible shield for protection, then I walk with determination and purpose down the courtyard to the chapel and into the prison library.

If anyone would have told me I would be starting a meditation program at a men's prison near Dallas, Texas, I would have thought they were bonkers, especially in the Bible Belt where meditation is still considered a bit strange. I recently learned that I am the only female in the entire state of Texas prison system who teaches meditation. There is only one male who teaches an Eastern based form of meditation. According to the National Institute of Corrections, on December 31, 2020, the number of incarcerated individuals in 64 State Prison facilities in Texas was 135,906.[1]

Doreena Durbin

With the amazing benefits and results of a daily meditation regimen, I feel this program should be offered in every prison facility in the country and beyond. During my 45 years of teaching meditation, this is the best and most rewarding class I have ever taught. The inmates come from all different backgrounds, various races, religions, and ages, all having unique life experiences. The daily onslaughts of prison life are difficult, so these programs are changing the lives of inmates from the inside out. This not only benefits the inmates but it also benefits the prison, the community, and the state of Texas. I am fortunate to be a part of this spiritual journey and transformation. There is an energetic exchange that takes place between teacher and students. At times, I feel that the inmates are teaching me more than I am teaching them. Everyone has something to learn and everyone has something to teach. When I am walking down the courtyard after teaching my classes, a sense of euphoria and paroxysms of joy surge through my body in a dance of lights. My **Prison Meditation Program** (PMP) needs to spread to prisons throughout the United States of America and around the world.

No Accidents

There are no accidents. As an optimist, I always look for the silver lining behind every dark cloud. The sun is always shining but it is "hidden" behind clouds. Call it karma, a learning experience, or simply something needed to wake me up, whenever something happens that knocks me off my feet, I know that it is for my own good. We all have life lessons and if we choose not to pay attention, the Universe will get our attention. We will keep getting confronted with situations until we wake up from our lower states of consciousness.

In November of 2023, while enjoying an evening with friends, I fell and broke my clavicle (collarbone). The details are not necessary. I was driven home and wanted to be left alone so I could figure out my next steps. I can generally tolerate pain but it was a little intense so I took an Advil and went to bed. I slept a couple of hours

2

and planned on calling someone in the morning to get a ride to Urgent Care. Having worked in the field of orthopedic surgery for over a decade, I had some understanding of the skeletal system. Also, being blessed with a strong intuition I knew I needed X-rays and suspected that I had a clavicle fracture. I was able to rest a few hours, even though I could not find a comfortable sleeping position. Early the next morning I called a friend who is a nurse and she offered to take me to Urgent Care. When I arrived, I told the doctor that I suspected that I had a clavicle fracture and to order X-rays to confirm my self diagnosis. She looked at me quizzically and I could almost "hear" her thinking, "How would you know? You're not a doctor." X-rays were taken and 15 minutes later she came back into the room and said... "You are right. It's a clavicle fracture!" Fortunately, I did not require surgery and my left, non-dominant shoulder was affected. I was sent home with an arm sling and pain meds and was told it would take about 6-8 weeks to heal. I was immobile. I couldn't drive, couldn't sleep comfortably or lift anything with two hands. I couldn't even open a bottle of water!

My awareness connected to Source energy was shining through the darkness to uncover what the Universe was trying to convey. Instead of feeling sorry for myself I asked my higher self, "Why did this accident happen? What do I need to learn from this experience?" I had complete trust that the Universe had a plan. Perhaps I needed to be more mindful. Maybe I should not have had that small glass of wine? I thought... "What am I going to do? I can't just sit around for the next 6-8 weeks doing nothing!" In that very moment I turned the negative into a positive. My inner voice shouted...**Write a book!** So, less than six hours after the accident, I took out my laptop and began typing with one finger, one letter at a time. I was so excited! The creative spark on the right side of my brain was very active as thoughts and ideas kept popping into my head faster than I could process them. I felt an inner push to get it all transferred from my brain onto the draft document. When I finally went to bed, more ideas continued

Doreena Durbin

popping into my head so fast, I couldn't sleep. I took advantage of that time, got up, made a cup of chamomile tea and added the new ideas that were swirling in my head. I continued typing until 4 AM. Here was my opportunity to take advantage of all my extra time by focusing on this, my first book! Unnecessary activities were curtailed.

I knew I could no longer walk my sweet 75 lb. dog Beto, and I did not have a fenced in yard. He had been my walking companion for nearly two years, helping me keep up with my exercise routine of walking 2-4 miles per day. I had fallen in love with him even though he was a handful, since he was always fixating on my invalid cat who was recovering from ear surgery. I rescued Beto from Animal Welfare, where I had been volunteering to walk dogs. I had hoped to make him a therapy dog and bring him to the prison to interact with the inmates. I had learned that dogs could offer emotional support. I had fallen a number of times when walking other dogs but Beto was very gentle until he saw a squirrel or a rabbit. Then he would dart full speed ahead pulling me down. He was much stronger than I and had the energy and strength of a pit bull. However, I knew I could not take a chance of suffering another fracture so I had to make a decision.

I must have been aligned with Universal energy when I put Beto's "Service Dog" harness on him and took him into Sam's Club with me. He loved going for rides and he especially liked snacking on the kibble that had fallen from the large bags of dog food onto the floor. He was a beautiful yellow lab mix with big expressive dark eyes surrounded by what looked like Egyptian eyeliner. I would often bring him with me into the big box stores and he always attracted lots of attention. Many people would stop to tell me their dog stories and show pictures on their phones. Some asked if they could pet him. If I sensed they had good energy, I would say, "Yes." If I felt they had negative energy, I would say, "No, he's in training." That particular day, as we walked down the aisle, a nice lady was coming towards us. She asked if she could pet him. I noticed she was looking at him with tears in her eyes so without hesitation, I said, "Yes." Then she asked if I could wait for her husband to catch up with her so he could see him too. When he came up to Beto, he knelt down to pet him. Beto put his head on the man's knee as if he already knew him. They said they had a dog that looked exactly like him that they had to put down. After a brief conversation, they said that if I ever needed to re-home him up to please consider them first. We exchanged phone numbers. One of the benefits of the spiritual path is that everything happens for our own good, if we pay attention. Little did I know that I would be calling this lovely couple several months after that synchronistic meeting. Knowing that I would no longer be able to walk him, I looked for their phone number and called to see if they were still interested. They were. Beto is now called Luke. I learned that Luke in the Bible was known as "the beloved healer."

I was scheduled to go to the prison several days after my accident and I knew I could not drive the 150 mile round trip in rush hour traffic. So, I called the Chaplain to let him know about my accident and that I would not be coming to the prison to teach my class for the next six weeks. I asked him to please notify the inmates on my behalf with my sincere apology. I knew that some of them who enjoyed the classes might be disappointed but now I needed to focus on myself, which gave me time to write this book.

CHAPTER 2
PRISON MEDITATION PROGRAM

In 2019, shortly after moving to Texas, I had the opportunity to teach meditation and mindfulness to a group of ex-convicts. I was working with a workforce development company which participated in community colleges and rehabilitation programs for exconvicts and homeless adults. Our program included trade and life skills to empower these people to be prepared for employment and for life on the outside. When the program ended, many of the men told me they wished they could have learned these valuable life changing meditation techniques and life skills while they had been incarcerated. They particularly liked the breathing practice, which aligns with the rhythmic pulsation of the breathing Universe. This was taught to me by a spiritual master. They said the practices could have saved them from getting emotionally triggered and reacting without awareness only to suffer the consequences of their actions. They discovered how quickly they were able to calm down and deescalate from their emotional reactions involving fear and anger after doing a couple rounds of the rhythmic breathing. The positive feedback I received from the ex-convicts sparked my interest to start a prison meditation program for "*captive*" audiences.

I fortuitously met the Reverend. He is a spiritual man who was instrumental in facilitating and linking me to the prison to initiate my meditation program. My intention was to provide inmates with a sense of hope and inner freedom. The Reverend and I shared a mutual interest in wanting to spiritually uplift the prison population and the community. I felt a spiritual bond and a connection with him. He had a warm, kind, friendly personality and my Spirit resonated with his. I consider the Reverend to be a beacon of light. My prison meditation program is under the umbrella of the Prison Ministries Program.

Meeting the Inmates

Prior to starting the program the Reverend invited me to the prison to meet with him and some of the inmates in the prison lobby. I signed in and was searched to ensure that I was not carrying contraband or anything else that was prohibited. He was kind and friendly and it was obvious that he was held in high esteem, and respected by the inmates and prison guards and employees who spoke to him along the way. I asked questions about what I needed to do to get my program launched. He provided me with names and phone numbers of the person in charge of the Volunteer program, and the Chaplain who was instrumental in assisting me with the process.

I assumed I would be introduced to a small group of inmates, but when we entered the Chapel I was surprised to see about 200 inmates sitting on white fold-up plastic chairs with their backs to me facing the stage. The Reverend motioned for me to sit in the back of the Chapel. Some inmates in the back rows turned around and saw me sitting behind a table. I noticed the word HOPE stenciled on the backs of their chairs and decided to incorporate that word in my presentation. I had not prepared anything, but I trusted that my words would be there after I was introduced. Four inmates were on the stage with musical instruments including a guitar, drums, bass guitar, and a keyboard. I felt comfortable and was happy to see them because they reminded me of my close knit musical family with three brothers and a sister. Based on my own experiences, I was aware that music can be a source of connectedness and healing. The inmates sat quietly and respectfully while listening to the Reverend speak. When he started his sermon the room lit up with positive energy. I was very impressed with his sermon. He was dynamic and powerful as the words of God flowed effortlessly offering hope and healing. I observed the inmates, listened with openness and awe to the inspiring sermon. I was reminded of Dr. Martin Luther King's sermons, which I had heard on radio and TV during the late sixties.

About an hour later, the Reverend called me up on the stage to introduce me. Being the only female in the room, I felt like I was in the spotlight. I took a deep breath and aligned myself with Universal energy. Having lived in and around big cities across America, I was doing my best to deal with the culture of Texas. In an effort to "fit in" I wore black jeans, a long sleeved Texas style blue/green flannel shirt and short boots with chunky heels. I gathered myself and walked with purpose past narrow rows of inmates on both sides of the aisle. I could feel the inmates following me with their eyes as I was passing by. I was confident my words would flow once I began speaking. They did. I was grateful that I had spent so much time on the stage playing music with my siblings during my childhood and into adulthood.

When I spoke, I felt Divinely inspired and trusted that my words would touch the hearts and minds of the men who were listening. I stated that I noticed the word HOPE on the backs of their chairs and thought it was a powerful message from the Universe that they should never give up. As Winston Churchill famously said during a Harrow's School speech in London, England in 1941 during WW2, "Never, never, never give up!" There is always hope. They may have experienced despair but that emotion is in the past, and nothing will change the past. The past is gone. The future is not here so the only thing they can do is to focus on the present moment, which is one of the main teachings of meditation and mindfulness. I spoke about meditation, life lessons, and our connection to Divinity and to each other. We may have different soul contracts and life lessons but each and every one of us is a child of God. No one is superior or inferior to anyone else. I shared that I was from the Southside of Chicago, at which point I heard hoots and hollers and saw raised fists coming from the middle and the back rows. They must have lived in Chicago. I asked for a show of hands for how many of them grew up in dysfunctional families. Nearly all of them raised their hands. I told them that we have something in common because I too grew up in a dysfunctional family. My siblings and I were raised as musicians by an authoritarian father who was a WW2 veteran. When one of us got into trouble we all suffered. I asked, "Does that sound familiar?" Many of them nodded or raised their hands.

Prisoners deal with punishment throughout the day. When one of their fellow inmates makes a mistake or gets into trouble, as a group they can all suffer. Lockdowns, prison checks, and quarantines can occur in their close quarters. As described by some of the inmates, those who are locked down become restless and get angry which can contribute to more altercations. When I finished, the guys were pleased. They stood up and clapped, giving me high fives as I walked back to my seat. When the program ended, I followed the Reverend out the back door of the Chapel. I was surprised to see all of the inmates lined up in the hallway standing against the wall. They were waiting for a guard to unlock the security gates so they could enter into the courtyard to go back to their dorms or elsewhere. As I walked past, nearly all of them shook my hand, gave me fist bumps and thanked me for coming. Some said they planned to sign up for my classes. One of them showed me a book about meditation he was reading. Another inmate showed me his name tag and asked me to remember him because he was planning on being the first to come to my class.

Doreena Durbin

Preparations

I spent the next six months preparing for my Prison Meditation Program. I needed to complete an application, provide documentation, make a proposal, and attend an orientation. Then in March of 2020 my son and his life partner planned a trip for us to go to Maui, Hawaii for a celebration. While there, I received a phone call from an officer at the prison informing me that my Prison Meditation Program had been approved to teach at prisons throughout the entire State of Texas. I was very excited!

When I returned home a few days later, the entire world changed due to the Covid virus. My program was put on hold and came to a screeching halt. I waited until the prison was safe and the virus was under control. While I was disappointed, I trusted that whatever the Universe had in store for me, was for my own good. As usual, I looked for positives in the negative situation. I let go and let God work out the details of the Divine plan. I felt a strong inner push to fulfill my Prison Meditation Program. I spent a great deal of time preparing and I wanted to provide this segment of humanity an opportunity to change their lives from the inside out. As a highly sensitive person and an empath my main concern was that I may have difficulty dealing with negative energy fields emanating around the prison and loud obnoxious sounds of clanging security gates, locks clamping, and shouts from guards. These assaults to my senses resound within the prison walls.

I was saddened to learn that some inmates contracted the Covid virus and never made it out of prison alive. I had to be patient and retreat within my home to keep myself safe. Finally, two years later, the prison reopened and volunteers were sent emails that we could resume our programs. This delay gave me an opportunity to be fully prepared for the inmates who would be attending my class. I was instructed to sign up for the mandatory orientation before I could begin my program.

10

Orientation

In 2022 I arrived early on the day of orientation and stood outside with other volunteers in the sweltering Texas sun. My body was already beginning to feel drained as the temperature continued to rise exceeding 90 degrees. I was fortunate to find a bit of shade on the side of a building. A couple of representatives from the Prison Volunteer Program walked up and down the line to ensure that we had completed the required documentation. Then we were scrutinized to make sure we had followed our emailed instructions about proper attire. We were instructed not to wear open toed shoes, sandals, or revealing clothing. Several women who were standing in line were turned away because they were wearing sandals or sleeveless blouses. We were frisked and body scanned and told to remove our shoes, cell phones, keys, and articles from our pockets.

We entered a large room filled with uncomfortable plastic folding chairs. After completing additional paperwork, we waited for the orientation leaders to speak with us about the taboos for volunteering in the prison system. We were shown several training videos and received detailed volunteer handbooks. One instruction was to be aware of our surroundings and to pay attention to inmate manipulation. Women were told that some male inmates had not seen a women's bare flesh for years and might be sexually aroused; therefore, women were advised to wear long sleeved shirts and long pants. Wearing white clothing was unacceptable because that was the color of the inmates' attire. We needed to be easily identified in the event a fight or altercation broke out. Hours later, after watching videos and live presentations, we had to pass an exam to ensure that we were educated and trained enough to begin our programs.

Near the end of orientation, I was exhausted and couldn't wait to get home. I looked up at the large wall clock and was shocked to see that it was nearly 9:00 pm! Nearly 14 hours had passed since I left my house earlier that day. I certainly did not expect

11

to be at the prison for more than a few hours. I was hoping to get out before nightfall, especially since I was unfamiliar with the dark roads adjacent to the prison. When I thought about the long commute home, I quickly stood up, grabbed my orientation packet, and began walking fast towards the door in the back of the large room. Others were still sitting in their uncomfortable chairs. All of a sudden my inner voice spoke loud and clear reprimanding me...*Where do you think you're going? You can't just get up and walk out! You're in prison!* I couldn't leave! Like the inmates, I was trapped and had to wait for security guards to unlock the multiple metal gates. I had a glimmer of insight as to how the inmates must have felt the first time they heard those heavy metal gates slam shut behind them. It was frightening! I thought... "I'm a free spirit! Nobody can control me or force me to stay!" I was concerned about how I would handle being locked up. It was a repulsive, scary feeling. I was accustomed to having the freedom to come and go as I pleased. Knowing that the freedoms of the incarcerated had been taken away from them, I wanted more than ever to provide them with a sense of hope and healing.

Trauma: Perpetrator or Victim

One of my life missions is to provide individuals with meditation techniques to support their spiritual and mental wellbeing and to offer new ways of thinking that will improve their lives with a sense of hope and happiness. Many of the inmates come from families with generational incarceration. When more positive energies are infused within the prison system, prison life can become a place of healing and redemption instead of a place of suffering and despair. Learning new ways of dealing with despair and anxiety improves mental and physical wellbeing. Increased awareness and more understanding uplift the inmates, offering an opportunity to turn their lives around. They deserve a chance for redemption. New ways of thinking and learning how to deal with negative thoughts allow more refined energy and light to filter in to replace the darkness. With meditation practices, they will have more awareness, the ability to use new skills, new ways of coping, and new understanding to support them for the rest of their lives.

Trauma is often associated with homelessness, sexual abuse, domestic violence, addictions, and witnessing crimes. Healing emotional wounds can be difficult for both the perpetrator and the victim. These can manifest as uncontrolled anger, fear, anxiety, nightmares, and Post Traumatic Stress Disorder (PTSD). Most inmates have been both perpetrators and victims of violence. Feelings of guilt, shame, and blame create patterns in the neural network of the brain that become rooted in the subconscious mind, patterns triggered by sensory input and outside events. Healing these emotional wounds can be difficult for both the perpetrator and the victim. There is evidence to suggest that intergenerational ancestral trauma passes to offspring through our DNA, altering genes. This science is called epigenetic, and is still developing. So if each and every one of us does our part to heal ourselves, future generations can benefit.

Some inmates are involved in crimes like armed robbery, or buying or selling drugs including heroin, cocaine, and methamphetamine. Others are incarcerated for assault with a deadly weapon, rape, or murder. Some of their crimes and offenses were committed in the heat of the moment, when "triggered," with emotions running high, thereby escalating the situation. I am not here to judge. Some offenders may have mental disorders like bipolar or schizophrenia while others were given unreasonable sentences based on their ethnicity or race. Many have the possibility of being released back into society after serving time. I am hoping to uplift and spiritually support them while they are incarcerated and before returning to their families and their societies. New life skills such as meditation and learning about the mind, and the physiological responses in the body will encourage them to stay *present* so they can catch themselves before reacting without awareness. A program of meditation can change their lives from the inside out. Learning new ways of dealing with the challenges in prison and how to

Doreena Durbin

handle life on the outside can turn their lives around, especially when faced with similar situations that sent them to prison. (I am cognizant that some crimes are so horrific that it is necessary to remove hardened criminals from society for the safety of societal members.)

My meditation program falls under Prison Ministry, which has Ministers, Chaplains, and Life Coaches giving offenders a chance to learn and voice their experiences while offering a sense of hope and healing. Many of the men who attend my classes are spiritually oriented with the intent to improve their lives. However, some of them may have just wanted to experience peace, silence, and air-conditioning! Continuing their punishment by keeping them locked up in never-ending cycles of punishment and blame will only perpetuate crime. What we do to one individual will affect another. We are all interconnected. My goal is to offer positive change to improve the lives of the incarcerated men one inmate at a time.

In my class, inmates learn how to meditate, and use a breathing technique that quickly calms them down whenever they are emotionally triggered. Love and light is infused into their beings and their surroundings. Hope replaces despair. Hate turns to love, offering new ways of perceiving and dealing with life's never ending challenges. Teaching inmates how to tap into their own inner beings whenever they feel disconnected or when they are feeling despair or disheartened helps them to help themselves. As my mother used to say, "God helps those who help themselves." As they are infusing meditation and prayer into daily activities, they awaken to new ideas and uplifting energies, which will change their vibrations and help them cope with the tense prison environment. These spiritual exercises can provide an opportunity to learn techniques that energetically and spiritually uplift them while they are serving time.

MEDITATE   Get an Inner Life!

Experience Freedom and Peace of Mind
through the Power of Meditation

- Meditation is not a religion and is not exclusive to any religion.
- Learn the difference between meditation and prayer.
- The goal of meditation is to achieve an inner state of peace.
- Increase awareness.
- Be fully alert and awake.

Freedom is Found Within

Learn how to quiet the mind by focusing on the breath to find peace. Meditation is simple and easy do. No special postures are required.

- Decrease anger and irritability
- Reduce fears and anxiety
- Combat depression
- Reduce physical and psychological pain
- Enhance a sense of wellbeing

Meditation is an inward journey and has been practiced for thousands of years in various forms by people of many different faiths and backgrounds.

Activate the ability of the mind and body to heal and purify itself. Connect with your inner selves.

When: April 4, April 18, May 9, May 23

Where: ▭State Prison - Chapel

Time: 3:00 - 4:30 pm

Instructor: Doreena

* Note to Inmates: For enrollment, you must send an I-60 to Chaplaincy.

My classes sometimes offer a little humor, which spontaneously arises before, during, or after the two hour time period. Humor can go a long way in changing the vibrations by infusing love, light, and joy into the inmates' lives. Those moments occur naturally. Uncovering our essence is the key to happiness and contentment. We unfold to a new understanding of how to get into the zone to reach the calm that is inherent within us, which supports us on our life journeys.

My Mission Begins

A feeling of excitement and trepidation was swirling in my head as I entered the prison to teach my meditation class. I was on a mission. The long walk down the prison courtyard was awaiting me as I was patted down and checked for restricted items. No phone, no purse, or bottle of water. Shoes removed and body scanned. After signing the volunteer book in the lobby I asked if someone could notify the prison Chaplain that I had arrived so he could unlock the last security gate. A female official behind a plexiglass window instructed me to put my driver's license through a little slotted window. She asked the purpose of my visit, checked prison records to ensure that I had been approved, and gave me a badge, which designated me as a Chapel Volunteer. Then I was allowed to enter through the next three security gates. Like the inmates, I was scrutinized and had to follow the rules.

During my walk, I could see several small groups of inmates standing around talking. I noticed that many of them had tattoos on their faces, heads, and arms. No one was wearing jewelry so I supposed that jewelry is not allowed in prison. Some inmates were walking between 24" wide yellow lines painted on the pavement in the courtyard. Guards were scattered throughout the prison yard monitoring the movements of the inmates. When inmates wandered too far outside of the lines, they were ordered to get back in line. When the inmates and I arrived at a security gate simultaneously, the guards instructed them to stop and step aside, allowing me to go through the gate first. A stern look or a shout from the guards was enough to keep them within the confines of the lines.

Most of the guards were friendly to me. The only problem I had was trying to understand their Nigerian and Kenyan accents when I needed directions or asked questions. I had to depend on them to call the Chaplain on my behalf, and to notify him that I was in the courtyard and to please unlock security gates and doors, especially since I was not allowed to carry a mobile phone. I learned to send the Chaplain a text notifying him that I had arrived in the parking lot. It sometimes took me as long as 20 minutes to get processed and screened upon entering the front lobby. When there were shift changes for the guards and employees, it took even longer. The delays in processing sometimes made me late for class. I didn't want to be late because it disrupts the schedule maintained by the Chaplain.

Once I left my driver's license with the person behind the plexiglass window, and received a volunteer pass, I was free to continue towards the chapel. After entering the courtyard, I noticed blue metal buildings with red doors on both sides of the courtyard. Each building has large white letters with a number. Those numbers are designated as dormitories. I walked past a building that had Diner signs on two separate doors. One diner was designated for the guards and the other diner for the inmates. The courtyard was half a mile long (round trip) from the front entrance to the end near the sidewalk that leads to the chapel. When I reached the last security gate, I spotted the steeple on top of the chapel. I had arrived! The Chaplain was waiting to unlock the metal gate for me. He welcomed me with a handshake and a smile. We walked to his office to discuss my personal schedule, the prison schedule, and the flier that I had been told to make to encourage inmates to sign up for my *Get An Inner Life: Meditate*" class. There must have been something in my flier that drew them in. Many of the inmates had never experienced meditation and signed up for my class out of a sense of curiosity. Perhaps the word *Meditate or Freedom* drew them in? The flier depicted a picture of the ocean and palm trees that I took on a recent trip to Maui. For me it represented peace and tranquility. I asked that it be posted around the prison to promote interest as to what my class entailed. Perhaps they were looking for new ways to uplift themselves by allowing positivity and higher vibrations to permeate their beings.

"It is so simple to be happy, yet so difficult to be simple." Gururaj

Living in the present moment is the key to happiness and bliss but that is easier said than done. Simplicity is profound and has tremendous power. The more complicated our lives, the more stress we have. As we meditate we move from fragmentation to integration, and a sense of wholeness is felt at a deep level. During the meditation process when you become the observer, you are using the mind as a tool to go to a place where tranquility and peace reside. They are always available for us to access. We get a sense of freedom when we can step aside from the mind, witness it with objectivity, and not be affected by what arises. Holding onto negative patterns of blaming and shaming will only keep us stuck and will leave a residue of toxic energies, which can lead to illness and disease. Whatever has happened does not require reliving those memories over and over again. Perhaps certain things had to happen to teach us lessons. Living in the present moment shifts our thinking from a futile sense of hopelessness to fresh new ways of thinking that bring more light into our lives. Meditation liberates us from the mind. As more light shines through, our lives begin to change and the power of Grace occurs naturally, offering hope and healing. Success in life is finding the peace that is inherent within. We must reach our center, which is nowhere else but within ourselves. That is where all polarities and separation cease and mental turmoil no longer exists. Accepting yourself is the first step in healing emotional wounds. The goal in life is to find freedom. Freedom is found through meditation, which doesn't require any development whatsoever. It only requires unfoldment. Getting an inner life while serving time in prison is the key to being able to tolerate prison life while learning new ways of dealing with restrictions and the lack of physical freedom.

Why Am I Writing This Book?

The inmates are the primary target audience and prison reform is one of my main concerns, which is necessary to uplift individuals and communities. Reducing crime and violence is the desired outcome of rehabilitation programs. In an effort to promote physical, mental, and spiritual wellbeing these types of programs are sorely needed for inmates around the world. This Prison Meditation Program offers insights into what the offenders are experiencing. I am hoping that the wisdom I developed in my lifetime, would be useful and instrumental in improving the lives of these individuals, not only while they are serving time, but also after they are released, thereby reducing the recidivism rates. Whether in an urban environment or in rural communities, the human experience is similar. We all seek peace, happiness, and freedom from the vicissitudes of life. Happiness is our ongoing quest.

Walk a mile in my shoes. This phrase elicits empathy and compassion. Giving inmates a new lease on life and a sense of hope can do wonders for their rehabilitation while spiritually uplifting them to increase their self esteem. As Jesus and the Dalai Lama taught, having compassion for others is the essence of Christianity and Buddhism. We treat others the way we want to be treated. We do not know the life stories and circumstances that led inmates to prison.

Inmate G. was in the hallway outside of the library when I arrived for my class. As I was waiting for the other inmates to arrive, I invited him in to chat. I began asking him questions about his role in the prison. He was setting up the microphone and sound system. He said he was grateful that his adoptive father had taught him about electronics. As an *Intuitive Empath,* I find it common for people, even total strangers, to share their life stories with me. Sometimes they just need to be heard so I am there to listen. I felt some sadness from this inmate and intuited that this man just needed a safe place to talk to release the pain that had been hidden inside of him. I learned that he has no memory of his mother. He recalls meeting his biological father for the first time when he was five. His father came to see him in a foster home or a social services setting and told him that this was the last time he would ever see him. He never explained why. The child was left with memories of his father and no memory about mother. The only thing he understood was they were not there for him. These life situations often manifest as feelings of abandonment, or feelings of not being good enough, which leave emotional scars and an energetic hole in the heart. He did not understand why other children had parents who loved and cared for them and he didn't.

Soon, he started acting out and getting into fights with his foster parents' older biological son and children at school. He was silently screaming for attention and just wanted love and acceptance. The only way the young boy was able to express his anger was by fighting. He continued getting into trouble and was left with deep emotional scars, which eventually landed him in prison. As he spoke, I perceived good energy emanating from him. His eyes were full of sorrow and regret. He appeared as someone who was dedicated to changing his life for the better as he was learning new coping mechanisms and new ways of overcoming challenges. I got the impression that he didn't get a fair shake in life. Some of the inmates have very sad and difficult life stories. I wonder what life lessons they need to learn to undo the damage that has been done to their psyches.

After he wound up in prison after years of serving time, he wrote the following letter to his brother whom he had offended. G continues to serve time at the prison doing his best to rehabilitate as he is learning valuable lessons of acceptance and forgiveness.

Family Letter from G, Serving 27 Years in a Texas Prison

What to tell you? Have I hurt you? Yeah. I did not physically, yet mentally and socially.

Yes, I have stolen from you too. Tit for tat right? Anyway, by what I have done the crimes I've committed in Texas brought embarrassment to you and the family and I'm not gonna go through the... *would have*, *could have*, *shouldn't*, and *should have*. We are both in our mid 50's. H. and J. are gone from this life. But I want you to know I've hated you and resented you for years. As I know you did me when your mom and dad adopted me. You were special and you knew it. I never wanted anything but a family to love me as H. and J. loved you. I'm not saying they did not love me. Yet there was always a difference and you looked at me as an enemy. I was not your enemy yet you fought me and did things that I got blamed for.

I no longer hate or resent you K. It has taken me many years to come to this point in my life. I am now being the man that God has been calling me to be, knowing my purpose in life now. Means too that I now know and understand that my God will not forgive unless I forgive people that have offended me.

I want you to know that God has created a spirit in me that has forgiven you K. of everything and I hope and pray that you will forgive me as well. K. I love you.

Your Brother, G.

Emotional wounds often leave deeper impressions in the mind than some physical injuries. These wounds can take many years, even a lifetime to heal. However, with spiritual practices, awareness increases and more light shines through the darkness revealing the truth behind negative events. With meditation, and increased awareness, objectivity and understanding are revealed. The memory is still there but it has less of an effect. The practitioner is taught to let go of thoughts. Holding onto thoughts and memories that lead to depression and emotional suffering is not life sustaining. Learning new ways of handling problems and rising above memories and negative thoughts can do wonders for our wellbeing. Over time, memories can dissipate leaving us with a sense of peace. Eventually with meditation practices, emotional pain can be reduced.

Self acceptance and taking responsibility for our own thoughts and actions is crucial for healing and wellbeing. Compassion, love, and acceptance are necessary if real change is to take place in individuals, societies, and our entire penal system. Prison resources that promote positive understanding result in positive change.

CHAPTER 3

MEDITATION OR RELIGION?

One of the common barriers in bringing a meditation program to prisons, universities, and to some segments of society where certain ideologies are ingrained in the culture, is the fear that meditation will conflict with faith or religion. In plain and simple terms, the answer is "No!" Meditation does not conflict with religion and is not specific to any one religion. According to the Religious Landscape Study in a A Pew Research meditation is practiced at least once a week by 49% of Evangelical Protestants.[2]

When you sit or lie down to meditate and turn your attention from the outer world to the peace and silence of the rich, expansive inner world, one of the first things you notice is that the breathing slows down significantly and becomes more shallow. Meditation is a simple easy way to get beyond thoughts into the present moment by using the breath, a visual object, or a mantra as a focal point. Experiencing peace of mind and being in a state of presence during the meditative state is a liberating experience. It has been said that the spiritual path is not for cowards. It takes courage to see and accept yourself just as you are, including the good, the bad, and the ugly. Letting go of fears of being scrutinized, criticized, and judged may be just what we need to awaken from our egoic minds. The power and expansive, freeing qualities of meditation can release negativity and fear provoking thoughts, which is crucial for our mental wellbeing.

What is the difference between meditation and prayer?

Prayer is when you speak to God...Meditation is when you listen.

Meditation teaches the practitioner to put their attention on their breathing and to stay in the present moment, with awareness, where there are no judgments, opinions, or name and form. Meditation is easy to do when using the proper techniques as taught by trained meditation teachers. As you go deeper, old memories and thoughts that have been stored away in the subconscious mind will surface. When those memories are revealed, you will see them with more clarity and objectivity. Instead of running away in fear, hiding your head in the sand, or evading thoughts buried deep inside, it is best to release them so negative or fearful thoughts don't take root. When negative thinking becomes habitual, it can settle in the body and manifest as an illness or disease.

The fear of shining light on the darkness and seeing yourself clearly, can be a bit frightening for some people. Their greatest fear is that their egos will be annihilated. Some call meditation the hero's path. Life experiences that have left deep impressions may take longer to heal but it is definitely worth the effort to uncover them and let them go. As we meditate we are unfolding to ourselves in an easy and effortless way. Learning how to let go of negative thoughts can take time, but it is the best way to achieve peace and happiness. Those who have the courage to peer through the darkness to witness the mind from a higher state of consciousness will see beauty and unconditional love for themselves and for others. The benefits can be immediately felt after returning to the waking state. A beautiful, peaceful, calm energy is experienced and emanates from your being as you feel uplifted and more compassionate.

In the words of Eckhart Tolle, "The primary cause of unhappiness is never the situation, but the thoughts about it: be aware of the thoughts you are thinking."

While you are meditating, others might be curious and want to know what you are doing. Those who are sensitive to energies might be able to perceive positive spiritual energy emanating from your being. Whatever the reason, it is important to consider it a distraction and if you can, after the disturbance, try to go back to your meditation; otherwise, it might leave you with nervous tension.

As you tune into the presence of Divinity, you will ultimately realize that everything in the Universe is a manifestation of the Creator. We come from One Source. With over eight billion people living in the world, it is unlikely that everyone will think or to be like us. We may be on different levels of consciousness or we might have different educational backgrounds and practice different religions; however, no one is superior or inferior to any other human being. We may have different life experiences, life paths, and ideologies but we are all interconnected. Choosing our individual paths that resonate with our beings will provide us with a sense of freedom to be who we really are. Be yourself! Prisons are not conducive to free spirits but through meditation and spiritual practices we can learn to rise above the restrictions in our minds and bodies, even while serving time.

CHAPTER 4
WALKING THE LINE

When I enter the prison courtyard there are lots of barbed razor wire security fences and yellow lines painted on the walkways spaced about two feet apart. Inmates follow each other closely one behind another, walking within the yellow lines. I hear the Johnny Cash song, "Walk the Line" playing in my head. The guards who are responsible for keeping them in line, sometimes shout at them if they step too far outside of the lines. I feel the negative energy of the inmates and get a sense of their emotional pain, frustration, and humiliation. I look at their faces and sometimes catch a glimpse of their eyes as I pass them along the way. Some smile or nod at me while trying to engage me in brief conversation. Depression is rampant amongst the inmates. Many of them relive memories and ruminate about the past. Some lose their loved ones while they are detained behind bars. If they choose to eat breakfast they must be up at 3:00 or 4:00 AM, otherwise they must wait for lunch. Some can sleep late while others who have programs to attend or roles to play, must get up early. The inmates share their plexiglass dorms with 55 other roommates. Lights are on 24/7 so even when they close their eyes to sleep, the lights remain on. Some inmates told me that in an effort to block out light to experience darkness, they tie a sock around their head to cover their eyes. Some say that they are sometimes awakened by guards who check to see if they are alive so at times they are pushed to make sure they are breathing.

With regular meditation practices, the vibrations and energy change in the inmates, and they emit and radiate a higher vibrational frequency. This energy is felt by everyone around them, especially by Highly Sensitive People. Valuable tools of meditation, contemplation, and prayer are readily available within oneself when uncovering our Divine spiritual essence. Learning new ways of coping while spending time in prison supports spiritual growth. When we align ourselves with strength, the Universe naturally supports us through synchronicity, grace, and divine protection. Our world is a projection of our collective consciousness. All people desire inner peace and harmony.

The Universe and Humanity

The Universe evolves no matter if we like it or not! Humans make mistakes whenever they are only concerned about personal gain or when their egos are involved. Some people react impulsively, and then try to blame others until the realization dawns that he or she participated in the offense. Objectivity and awareness are useful in helping us see different sides and perspectives of a situation. No one can push their ideas on others unless there is a mutual agreement. During the meditative state we treat thoughts as neutral without trying to control them in any way. We simply watch our thoughts come and go and do not get caught up in them. Aggression is our way of trying to get others to bend to our wishes. There is a flow and spontaneity that brings adventure into our lives. People fear what they don't know or understand. As we evolve, the world is evolving too. Change occurs in every single moment. Nothing ever stays the same. As the saying goes… "You can never step into the same river twice." Attachment to the way that things were, only causes suffering and emotional pain. We must let go and allow ourselves to feel our connection with Source energy and learn how to live in the present moment.

We are one Unity Consciousness separated from each other by distance, time, or space. We are energetically and biologically drawn to others at the soul level. Like attracts like. Negative thoughts attract negative people and situations, whereas positive thoughts attract positivity and uplifting relationships. We attract people, situations, and circumstances into our lives based on our vibrational frequency. The saying that, "I am responsible for everything that happens to me" is necessary for us to stop blaming others. We are the masters of our lives. Taking responsibility for our actions knowing that we cannot blame others can release us from ruminating about things we cannot change. Mystics have said that we make soul contracts with our Creator prior to taking birth, and we experience certain things that are put on our paths for the purpose of teaching us certain life lessons. Having gratitude for being alive and for having a place to sleep with a roof over our heads and food to eat (even if it's not fit for a king) is a blessing.

Some people may have been born into impoverished families or circumstances, lacking the basic necessities of life, where food was scarce and affordable housing was unavailable. Some may have been born into wealthy families and never had to worry about where their next meal was coming from. We live in our own little worlds where we play various roles but in reality we are all the same. Human beings are trying to survive in the best way we know. Nobody is better than another, regardless of job or career. I learned that from my parents. Having grown up in the world of music as an entertainer, I met lots of people. Therefore, I am very comfortable communicating with people from various walks of life. I always felt that the only differences between me and others were our roles, careers, educational backgrounds, or socioeconomic status. Otherwise, we are all from the *Homosapien sapien* species trying to do the best we can to survive, seek happiness, and prosper. I learned that whatever role we play, it is neither good nor bad. It is just a role: doctor, lawyer, teacher, musician, or inmate. Suffering occurs when we become attached to our roles. We all have unique life stories. We may have regrets but there is nothing we can do except apologize if necessary, and try to make amends. Drugs and alcohol may have been involved, which would have affected our judgment. I encourage all inmates who are struggling with addictions to take full advantage of the prison resources: Alcoholics Anonymous, Narcotics Anonymous, educational resources, and counselors who offer emotional and spiritual support.

As humans we are always seeking love and joy, which are inherently within us. When we don't find it within, we search outside of ourselves. Finding inner joy and doing spiritual practices and learning to quiet the monkey mind leads us to the power that resides within our beings. It is not until we link up with our inner power that we realize that seeking temporary happiness through external means such as drugs or alcohol keeps us trapped into habitual negative cycles, which promotes addictions. Unfortunately, these temporary highs are not going to provide us with real joy. Peace and happiness found during meditation is longer lasting.

Money, possessions, and fame do not define us. They do not bring us permanent happiness. They may provide temporary happiness but for genuine long-term happiness, we must unfold to the goodness and joy we have inside of ourselves. The rich and famous suffer depression just like everyone else. Offering a few words of encouragement and having a little compassion and understanding can do wonders to uplift another's spirit. This can be done in small ways, even in prison. When we are on our deathbeds we do not think..."Oh, I wish I would have bought a bigger house or driven a nicer car." These are ego boosters and can keep us on a path of greed while bolstering our egos. When we reach the end of our lives, money and possessions are meaningless. We cannot take them with us when we pass into the next realm, no matter how hard we worked or how many years we spent accumulating possessions and wealth. When our time is up, we do not regret spending more time at work. Instead, we think... "I wish I would have spent more time with my loved ones telling them how much I love them."

Doreena Durbin

At the end of my musical career, my husband and I attended a gathering at a golf country club across the street from our home in Las Vegas, Nevada. We brought our adorable three year old daughter with us. A number of celebrities were there, including Sammy Davis Jr. When he saw our daughter, he squatted down on the ground to give her a hug. When he stood up he began talking with me saying that my husband was very fortunate to have both of us in his life. I assumed he had a few too many drinks because he was very emotional as he cried on my shoulder. He told me that he was in the middle of another divorce with his second wife. I listened with compassion as he shared his story. He spoke about how depressed he was to have another failed marriage. Growing up in the world of entertainment, it was not unusual for me to encounter celebrities. Listening to Sammy's story demonstrated to me that money and fame cannot buy love and happiness. Most people have had to deal with severed relationships. We are all one humanity living similar experiences as we seek love and happiness.

CHAPTER 5
DIVINITY RESIDES WITHIN

With meditation and spiritual practices we plug into our Divine inner selves, and experience a sense of freedom through Unity Consciousness. The tools are already there; we just need to learn how to use them. God is omnipresent and eternal and exists in us and everything around us. Meditation practices teach you how to turn your attention inward to access the expansive rich inner world where peace and tranquility reside. Meditation is not an intellectual exercise. Nor is it escapism. Instead, it is experiential. Learning from a trained meditation teacher with access to ancient practices where you are guided step-by-step into the inner realms of love and light, is Divinity itself. An expansion of awareness can open new pathways to co-create with the Universe as we unfold to stability, strength, and Grace. Overcoming challenges while fulfilling your life lessons are part of the Divine plan. Perhaps the ego has become inflated and lessons of humility are necessary to achieve balance. Striving to live a balanced spiritual life while tolerating the onslaughts of prison provides meaning and a deeper understanding while serving time. Inmates change from the inside out as they unfold naturally to their inner selves and connect with the One Source. When our minds and bodies are infused with pure positive energy, light replaces darkness and we become happier and more content. Transformation and awakening occurs as we unfold to our higher selves. You can never go back into the past, except in your mind. Your former self is gone and will never return. It is important to do what you can to repair the damage that has been done. Healing relationships is part of the process and is important for us to move on. Having a commitment to improve and grow from past experiences can set us free from holding onto hurt, anger, and unlawful acts of crime.

With the benefits of increased awareness, inmates are less likely to reoffend. Many of them did not have good role models growing up. Perhaps they grew up without parents in very difficult, abusive environments. Some of them followed in the footsteps of their ancestors where family members also spent time in prison. Nearly everyone has emotional and ancestral wounds. Hope and healing are important for incarcerated individuals, so if or when they are released they can make positive contributions and become valuable members in society. They may serve humanity by being a source of hope and healing while teaching others who might be tempted to go down the wrong path. Unfortunately, people who lack compassion or have fear are more likely to treat them differently and hold them to their crimes. Thus they continue to be punished for their misdeeds.

Shortly after birth, we think the world revolves around us and we look for satisfaction as we seek our mother's milk for nourishment. As we begin to engage with other people, we discover that we are not alone. We become conscious that we share our little egocentric worlds with other people in our households. We learn to share our world with siblings, cousins, family, and friends. Our little world gets bigger and includes not only people but also animals. In reality, we are just a tiny part of an incomprehensible Universe.

Cosmic evolution unfolds and we evolve. It is part of the process of life. Trees, for example, start from seeds and with water, sun, and minerals grow into beautiful expressions of nature. The cycles of life and death continue even after the tree is no longer viable. As science continues to evolve and telescopes become bigger and more powerful, we learn that the Universe has 100 billion galaxies. The more we learn, the more we feel like a tiny speck in the Universe. Yet, we learn that we are all living miracles. Our intricate, amazing bodies have approximately 30 trillion cells (too much for the mind to fathom). The human brain has approximately 86 billion neurons and each neuron can make connections with 1000 other neurons.[3] Our paths are all unique and different and our souls are eternal and free. There is an adventure around every corner.

"You are here to enable the divine purpose of the Universe to unfold. That is how important you are! We are here to learn life lessons. We fit into the Grand Design." Eckhart Tolle

CHAPTER 6
ACCEPTANCE

Ok, I'm in prison. Now what?

The element of acceptance comes into play here. In order to grow and evolve sometimes we must take a step back and reevaluate our lives. Where did we go wrong? Where are we are going? Is there anything we need to do differently before getting out of this hell hole we have been living in? Before getting entangled in the razor wire, think about what we need to learn from our experiences. None of us can judge another person's life path, but when their life paths are juxtaposed or connected to our own, we find ourselves getting involved. They might be just what we need to help break bad habits or life cycles of abusing our bodies with temporary highs and lows. What is good for one person may not be good for another. We have our own life lessons to become better human beings. No one knows what experiences another had prior to incarceration that has caused emotional or physical pain.

How we choose to direct or focus attention can create a sense of peace and tranquility even in the most difficult circumstances. Getting into thought wormholes of blame and shame will keep us in negative cycles. They are useless and will not change anything. Forget about the past! It is gone and the future is not yet here! The present moment is all we have so why waste time on nebulous fears and negative thoughts? Some incarcerated individuals may have been misjudged or have been victims of circumstances and wound up in prison. Society is not always fair. Some of the lessons we learn for our own spiritual growth are necessary to move us forward. Acceptance is needed in order to learn certain lessons.

Ruminating about what we could have done differently will not change the outcome, but learning how to let go and let our Creator work out the details, is an important step, which can set us free. Being imprisoned physically and mentally while serving time behind iron bars and barbed wire is a double whammy, where you are stuck in a hellish nightmare reliving negative memories that cannot change. What good does that do? Do those thoughts and memories make you feel any better? Rising above challenges and striving to change your life for the better cannot be done until you come to terms with the past and accept yourself just as you are. Acceptance is the key. Find the good in your life by objectification, which happens during meditation. Perhaps the only way to evolve is by being forced to spend some time locked away from others in society.

My Experience of Jail

My only experience of jail was when I was 18 years old. I was detained for a few hours at a police station on the Southside of Chicago. I didn't do anything wrong but I was at the wrong place at the wrong time and with the wrong group. My friend and I were typical teenagers who were just looking for an exciting experience in the big city. We were invited to attend a party with an older friend who asked if we could pick him up along the way. He saw a liquor store and asked me to pull over so he could run in to get some alcohol for the party. I didn't have the skills to consider the consequences of my actions. My friend and I had no desire to imbibe. We were just looking forward to meeting some new people and having a good time. Suddenly my car was surrounded by three police cars with flashing blue lights and a couple of unidentified vehicles. The police shone bright flashlights into my car and in my eyes. My heart was palpitating. Fear surged throughout my body as I responded to the assault.

As the police were checking our driver's licenses and looking inside my car, I noticed my older male friend coming out from the liquor store with a small brown paper bag holding a bottle of alcohol. The police already knew that my girlfriend and I were underage and they might have assumed that he was buying the liquor for us. One of the police officers snatched the bag, opened the bottle and took a big swig. He said, "Ok, we got them on this!" In retrospect, I believe they needed an excuse to bring us in for questioning. They shoved my friend and me into one of the police cars and our male companion into another. We were hauled into the nearest police station, which happened to be in a very bad, crime-ridden neighborhood. As we were being led into the interrogation room, we witnessed an African American man being beaten by a white police officer. The cop looked at us and sneered while saying, "This is what is going to happen to you if you don't cooperate." During the interrogation they dumped the contents of my purse on the table, searching for drugs or a weapon. They found a bottle of Darvon (pain meds) in my purse that had been given to me by a nurse at my workplace for my abscessed tooth. My friend and I were brought into another room to be strip searched by a female officer while they took our male friend to another room to be interrogated separately.

They asked for our phone numbers so they could call our parents. I gave them the wrong number, which rang but nobody answered. My friend gave them her correct phone number and her father answered. I call it "Divine intervention" because her father lived across the street from the Police Lieutenant at that police station. We were held for what seemed like an eternity, but it was probably only a few hours as they sent the pain meds to be analyzed. Then we were set free because they couldn't find any reason to hold us. They said the Lieutenant had a major part to play in our release, thanks to my friend's father. I thanked God for keeping me protected during that frightening experience. In retrospect, perhaps I needed that early life experience so I could have some understanding and a glimpse of what the inmates might have experienced during their arrests and subsequent incarceration(s).

Early in my spiritual journey, I went to a workshop in Las Vegas that was led by a meditation instructor. He gave me a sheet of paper, with the words that said,

"Everything that happens to me is caused by me." I carried it around with me for years. Every time I tried to blame someone, I would be reminded that I am responsible for my hurt, anger, blame, and shame. At first those words made me angry and I questioned the validity of this statement. I know that we create our own reality but this concept created controversy in my mind. I thought… "What about innocent victims and children who have been physically and emotionally abused? How could that be true?" I came to learn to become more independent and not rely on others to "save me." Seeing myself as co-creator with the Universe, has provided me with understanding and empathy for the suffering of others. Finding forgiveness is very difficult but it can be done when we think about what might have occurred in the abuser's life that led him or her to commit crimes or to do the things they did. Rising above negativity with understanding, love, compassion, and forgiveness will empower and elevate us vibrationally. We are not doing that for others. We are doing it for ourselves.

During incarceration, inmates can seek relationships and opportunities to turn their lives around while also finding ways to uplift and teach one another. Working through relationship issues is a necessary step to let go of our egos, which get bruised from time to time. Disentangling ourselves from the energetic bonds that delay our spiritual progress can be achieved with courage and grace. When people in our environment are difficult, they are providing us with opportunities to see our faults and frailties. When we develop the courage to face them, then we remove the barriers that keep us from experiencing our real selves. Thank them, because they might be our greatest teachers. As Jesus said on the cross, "Father, forgive them, they know not what they do."

Finding Humor in the Prison Environment

According to the inmates who come to my classes, prison life is not easy. There is no privacy. Some inmates are given prison jobs and various roles. Many of them attend church services or take advantage of resources provided by volunteers. They also watch TV and some have tablet devices to hear podcasts or music. Incarceration can cause psychological problems such as self condemnation, guilt, and low self esteem. I can imagine there must be some snoring and that might encourage an inmate to have a desire to take a pillow and do the unthinkable. During one of my first classes, one of the guys asked if they could meditate while lying down on the floor. I said they could but if they want to be more comfortable, I suggested that they bring their own pillows. They looked at each other and broke into laughter. It immediately dawned on me as to why they were laughing, and they began poking fun at the idea that the guards would allow them to bring pillows from their dorms. I laughed along with them once the absurdity of my comment dawned upon me. Bringing pillows is not a good idea in prison unless a guard is present! I was reminded of my brothers who would tease me when I said something stupid or absurd. I would be ridiculed and teased for years. In that moment of jest, I felt like these inmates were my brothers. I felt a sense of lightness and joy filling the room as we all laughed together. I decided that we should continue finding moments of joy during our classes even if it's at my own expense. During my 1-2 hour drive home I have time to reflect on what occurred during the class. I realize that I need to continue incorporating some happiness and joy into my classes. Laughter releases biochemicals in the brain as endorphins, serotonin, and dopamine flood the body.

Anxiety and Depression

Inmates may feel anxiety and depression, leaving them feeling irritable, hostile, and hyper vigilant. The prison experience can be overwhelming. With increased awareness, meditators often report that they are able to observe their thoughts with more clarity. They may feel higher vibrations and frequencies that resonate with their beings. As they turn their attention away from anxiety-producing thoughts to inner solitude, and embrace thoughts of love and joy, veils of darkness are lifted and more light shines through. Ancestral wounds are healed, and emotional pain and anger dissipate as lighter vibrations and frequencies permeate their bodies and minds. A quality meditation program with a trained instructor who can guide them to their inner beings offers the inmates a sense of hope and freedom.

Some inmates have PTSD, which may cause nightmares or unwelcome memories. Several guys told me that they sometimes have nightmares. They were shocked when I shared what my teacher used to tell his students. He would say, "Have more." He said it helps them to release toxins from the mind.

As part of the animal kingdom, we humans feel instinct and adrenaline surge through our bodies as a defense mechanism, which is necessary for our survival. Being fully aware of the fight or flight syndrome following an adrenaline rush is a valuable tool for not reacting prematurely. Some of us live in danger zones where fear and anger are the norms rather than the exceptions. Meditation and breathing practices help diffuse negative energies, keeping us from harm in dangerous situations. When fear and anger arise, the infusion of positive energy lessens impulsivity.

Doreena Durbin

Lockdowns can be unbearable for most inmates. As one inmate described it, the guys can go "stir crazy," especially when the lockdown is long. However, he also told me because he has experience with meditation he is actually benefiting from the lockdown(s). See his story in Chapter 19 entitled, **"Personal Experiences of Inmates."**

CHAPTER 7
MEDITATION IN PRISON

Utilizing meditation programs and spiritual techniques in prison is not a new phenomenon. Some programs, such as the *Prison Ashram Project (1973), Lozoff, B. S., in cooperation with Ram Das* are being used in prisons throughout the U.S. as a way to encourage prisoners to turn their attention inward to their real selves and not their ego selves.[4] The inmates benefit by learning how to control their emotions and the prison benefits with fewer incidents of violence. Meditation helps inmates release stress and develop self awareness, so that when conflicts and violent situations occur, the likelihood of engaging can be curtailed. Observing thoughts and having the ability to recognize the subtle nuances that occur in the body before one reacts impulsively is a gift, and is a powerful internal mechanism for reducing stress, thereby reducing violence. Our intuitive faculties increase with awareness.

Finding a conducive time and place to meditate that is free from distractions in a chaotic prison environment can be challenging. Yelling inmates and guards, television, radio, clinging chains, and clanging slamming doors can compete with the inmates' ability to quiet the mind and relax the body. However, certain meditation techniques can offer solace where distractions do not disturb the meditators' body and mind.

41

Doreena Durbin

Meditation has existed for thousands of years in various forms and in many cultures around the world. Nearly all religions practice some form of meditation. It has often been associated with Eastern religions but today it is practiced by people who do not follow any traditional religion. People are free to practice and get the benefits without having to join a traditional religious organization. However, if they practice any religion, meditation can deepen their experiences.

During the 1970s in America, many people had not taken meditation seriously and some even considered it a fringe religion, not understanding that meditation is not a religion. Most religions around the world use meditation, prayer, or chanting as part of their spiritual practices. There is something healing about chants and prayers. They take the mind off of negativity and allow a purification to neutralize the mind of toxicity.

Meditation is often depicted as someone sitting in a cross legged position with their thumb and forefinger together. These yogic poses are not necessary, especially in a prison setting since it can be very difficult to find a conducive spot to meditate. Other inmates and guards sometimes disrupt the meditator out of curiosity as to what they are doing. Depending on their sensitivity, they may feel peace emanating from the inmate and may be wondering how they remain calm in the midst of chaos. Sitting in a chair or lying in bed is most conducive for inmates to meditate. Walking meditation can also be achieved by staying present with each and every step. Meditation enriches our lives as we unfold to a greater sense of awareness while staying alert and in the present moment. The aim of meditation is to allow us to experience Divine contemplation and the presence of God. Quiet solitary moments can elicit spiritual growth. In the state of meditation we access the subtler levels of our minds. Based on my own meditative experiences, we might feel a stronger connection with others in our surroundings. An open heart encourages compassion and empathy.

Personal Strengths and Challenges

After decades of practicing and teaching meditation, I was eager to begin teaching inmates the powerful ancient meditation techniques that have literally changed my life. I had been assured that a prison guard would be outside the room as a measure of safety and security. My main concern was how I would handle dealing with the potentially difficult prison environment where negative energies were rampant. I have learned that navigating life as an empath with my highly sensitive nature is both a blessing and a curse. Empaths are affected by people around them. They absorb thoughts, emotions, and energy. Being in close proximity with large groups of people with loud talking and obnoxious sounds where negative energies are heightened, is an assault to my senses. Spending too much time in certain environments with negative energy or electromagnetic waves, can make an empath feel nauseous or physically drained. For me, even touching an object in resale shops can have that effect, especially if it was in the household or worn by someone who had very negative violent, angry energy! The positive aspect of being an empath is having a strong intuition. I learned to be vigilant while living in Chicago. Paying attention to gut feelings and my surroundings is essential when faced with difficult or potentially harmful situations or people. I had learned some street smarts when in threatening situations. I sometimes feel like I have a guardian angel by my side.

I was curious about what laws the inmates had broken that landed them in prison, but I did not want to focus on negatives or their bad behavior. Instead, I wanted to focus on their goodness and their strengths. Everyone has made bad choices from time to time, especially during the teen years. Getting caught up in drugs or alcohol was normal behavior in some families and social circles, including in show business, which is how I grew up. Based on my own experience, I find the inmates to be likable and respectful. They don't even curse in front of me, which is atypical for men in prison. My intent was to direct the classes to whatever topics my intuition told me would be most beneficial for their needs. As I get to know them, I am discovering that the guys who are attracted to my class have a spiritual quality about them; otherwise they would not be there. At times, I am in awe of their spirits, which I am witnessing unfold as they evolve. Incorporating whatever religion they are following in combination with meditation and the new techniques they are learning, will help them reach beyond their current restrictions and bondage. I am there to support their spiritual unfoldment.

We are all sparks of the Divine. Incarcerated individuals in jails, and federal and state prisons, have had their freedom taken away due to their crimes. A big part of their recovery is the healing of ancestral wounds involving alcohol and drugs, which have caused separations and discord amongst familial and societal members. It comes as no surprise that many of the incarcerated men came from dysfunctional families where it was common for generations—parents, grandparents, and others—to serve time in prison. As we grow spiritually we begin to realize that we are one humanity under one Creator and we each have the power to break cycles that are not conducive to our wellbeing. Once we come to the realization that whatever we do to others, we do to ourselves, real healing begins.

Like drops in the ocean we are all part of the same ocean and the One Source. We are heirs of God and everyone is worthy and valued. God doesn't differentiate between the worthy and unworthy. Heaven and hell are experienced right here on earth. Cataclysmic earthquakes, tornadoes, floods, and fires can make us feel like we are in hell. Having a strong spiritual inner core provides us with a stable foundation so that whatever happens to us becomes part of our life experience. It is more comforting to view each other as fellow travelers on this earth, instead of seeing each other as rivals or enemies. The best thing we can do is to heal our divisions and experience Oneness through integration rather than fragmentation. When we live our lives harboring hate, we become mistrustful, fearful, and angry. Focusing on our differences only divides and separates us. We must focus on our strengths and the link that ties us all together. Love is the highest form of primal human emotion; fear is the lowest. When we can see Divinity in everyone, regardless of ideologies or race, our diverse backgrounds merge into a myriad of beautiful colors.

As inmates learn new ways of coping and dealing with stress, they have the opportunity to improve their lives while serving time. Having a strong sense of spiritual support as inmates are preparing to assimilate back into society is comforting, necessary, and beneficial. When incarcerated individuals are released, their focus shifts from others controlling their lives to making their own decisions and being responsible for themselves and others in their families and communities. It is important for inmates to take advantage of the programs available to them in prison. Life is what we make it. Once our basic needs are met, such as housing, working, and taking responsibility for ourselves and our families, then we are on the road to recovery. Life challenges can be daunting but can also be a source of love and strength when everyone is doing their part to make our lives and the world a better place.

Many societal changes take place during a period of incarceration. The longer you are incarcerated the more you will experience challenges, especially when assimilating in the world. New technologies such as AI are quickly replacing antiquated technology, which may create stress for some, depending on their job requirements. We may find that the younger generation have more computer and technological skills than most adults. However, there are programs that can teach about computers and technology. Do not give up! Find the opportunities inherent in the challenges.

Inmates who continue their meditation and spiritual practices, will find that an inner energetic shift provides them with a sense of stability and strength. As they begin to feel more connected to their inner beings, they will be able to surmount whatever challenges they face with grace and dignity, and have a sense that no matter what happens to them, they will be ok. Having a sense of balance is an important step in this phase. When realization and acceptance all of life experiences are worthy and are part of the Divine plan, an element of acceptance is experienced. Self esteem increases when you pay it forward and give back to society. A sense of worthiness and value deserves respect and admiration.

Meditation and spiritual practices are positive ways to energetically shield inmates from the daily insults or assaults from guards and other inmates, which can trigger their emotions and defense mechanisms. With increased awareness impulsivity decreases and the ability to tune into inner guidance, intuition, and gut feelings increases. With practice, inmates will have a new sense of wellbeing and optimism. Stress levels will drop when new ways of finding peace and equanimity emerge. Learning how to be aware of thoughts and feelings prior to reacting is a valuable tool, and can be the difference between getting an early release or spending additional time behind bars. Living in the challenging prison environment can increase the possibility for lashing out at others with emotional outbursts and anger, where the potential for violence is high. Words spoken in anger often provoke the inmates and encourage negative reactions. Teaching inmates to be mindful when they feel an adrenaline rush when the fight or flight response is activated is very important. Learning to catch themselves from speaking out or reacting prematurely, or doing something they may later regret is a valuable gift. Learning to draw upon pure positive energy by connecting with our inner spirits and infusing light and positive energy into our thoughts and actions awakens us to a new sense of reality. As we awaken to pure positive refined energy in the cells of our bodies, prison cells dissipate and recede.

CHAPTER 8
FREEDOM

What is freedom? Freedom signifies having the right to speak, think, or act in whatever way we want without hindrance or restraint. Freedom is a state of independence where there are no restrictions. All humans worldwide, regardless of age, race, creed, or social status seek happiness and freedom from mental, physical, and emotional suffering. Taking responsibility for our thoughts, words, and deeds are the first steps to finding freedom. Emotional imprisonment can make one feel as if they are in a living nightmare or hell. Freedom is found within. All animals seek freedom. Animals caged for their entire lives is one of the saddest things I have ever encountered. I recall on a visit to India, seeing a bear with a rope around his neck standing upright and being walked around by men looking to make a few rupees. That is not God's plan for animals. They love and deserve freedom. As an empath I am so saddened for their plight, especially since humans sometimes abuse animals for power, control, or money. Elephants who are chained for years for circus acts are the most heartbreaking. What a horrible way to treat God's creatures!

Are you free? Can you be free in prison? 99% of people in the world live in self created bondage, even after release. In reality we are free to think however we want. These questions were in my mind as I began to think about the topic for my next class. I learned that State prisons such as this one were more dangerous than Federal prisons, where inmates are generally less violent.

State prisons typically house criminals who have committed murder, rape, or other violent crimes. People who are serving time in prison have had their freedom taken away as a result of bad choices or decisions they had made. Unfortunately, some of the people who are incarcerated are innocent and have to serve time for crime(s) they did not commit. Serving time can be a dehumanizing experience. Most of us at one time or another had made bad decisions and poor choices, especially during the teen years when the frontal cortex, the part of the brain responsible for reasoning, judgment, and impulse control, is impaired and not fully developed. Teens have difficulty thinking of consequences for their actions and sometimes find themselves in situations they later regret. Taking responsibility for our actions is necessary for our personal and spiritual growth. Awareness is a gift that can keep us out of trouble. It can also help inmates tolerate the prison experience.

Nature is Healing

Being in the midst of nature where we are surrounded by trees, a babbling brook, and wildlife can be wonderful experiences for healing our bodies and minds. Our troubles dissipate when we surround ourselves with the healing energy of nature. Listening to the melodies of birds, frogs, and crickets chirping resonates with our beings. Unfortunately, depending on the prison environment, the inmates may only be able to see a small part of nature. But even if they only see a small portion of the sky and stars, or a tree, they can still conjure up memories of past experiences of watching a beautiful sunset or observing the waves of an ocean, to align their spirits with nature.

No one can take away our spirits! Our spirits are forever free even if we are incarcerated. Meditation is not book knowledge. It is an actual experience. As we fit meditation practices into our daily lives, our understanding deepens and harmony results. When we experience peace within ourselves, anxieties and problems seem to melt away. Then a sense of freedom is experienced. Anxieties and fears dissipate when in the presence of God.

When we look up at the vast night sky and see thousands of bright stars, we feel very small and insignificant. Because our bodies are made of the same elements as stars, we are part of the quantum field made of atoms and molecules. Others might make us feel small and insignificant, but in reality, we are as vast as the Universe. Subatomic particles and atoms are 99% space and energy. In the quantum world the infinite Universe is not fixed but instead consists of swirls of energy. In the subatomic world, when we observe and focus our attention on the location of an electron, the electron changes location, which means that as we interact with the world around us, our thoughts can influence the movement of energy. We just have to realize the vastness of our beings. Humans, stars, and galaxies and everything in the Universe are connected to invisible energy. Our beings and our thoughts are interconnected beyond space and time. Fear freezes us and keeps us trapped in nebulous thought patterns of unreality. Feeling the Oneness of ourselves with the Universe is a vastly freeing experience.

I am hopeful that the spiritual energies of the guys in my class will have a positive effect throughout the prison as more and more inmates meditate. When our attention is turned from the outer world to the rich blissful inner world, upon returning to the waking state, we bring back peace and tranquility. When we tap into our source of power and knowingness, fear and anger dissipate as awareness increases. Going beyond the mind into the superconscious level or universal mind is a very simple, yet powerful way to tap into our own inner beings. That is why sages often advise to "Be in the world but not of the world." Getting caught up in worldly activities can drag us down and keep us stuck in ruts, and get us back to pre-incarceration states. We must make wise decisions to stay out of situations that can repeat cycles in states of unawareness. We have free will so we can

Doreena Durbin

choose how we live in the world, and remain unaffected by the challenges of life. Training the mind so you are not distracted by thoughts during the meditative state prepares you for life on the outside. As your own energies become more elevated and refined, you will automatically be drawn to people and events that support your wellbeing.

I believe that our higher selves make soul contracts with other beings to teach us various life lessons. That is why some people we meet are like magnets and we feel like we know each other or have déjà vu experiences. On the other hand, we are repelled by certain relationships. Everyone has something to teach and everyone has something to learn. Having a sense of gratitude for difficult relationships that have ended is necessary for our soul's development. Many of us find ourselves in difficult circumstances but when we look back, we can see how they provided us with opportunities to learn life lessons. Some people have superiority issues and resentment for people in society who are from different races or cultures. As my ancestors would say, put yourself in the moccasins or shoes of another. Be compassionate, kind, and loving. Being born in black, brown, yellow, red, or white skin makes no difference whatsoever to the Creator. This includes people from the LGBTQ communities. Discrimination comes from small, limited, fearful minds who stubbornly hold onto antiquated ideas with fears of being replaced by other human beings. Love and compassion are the most powerful human characteristics we have. Meditation helps break through barriers of limitation into a sense of freedom.

Perhaps we need to learn lessons of poverty, greed, or humility if we are born in families who live in lower socioeconomic segments of society. Honoring all beings and having mutual respect for all people, regardless of their race or monetary status, will make our world a better place. In God's eyes, no human being is more superior or inferior to another human being. Harboring hate or anger about people from various races or from certain segments of society can keep us stuck. Once we realize that our thoughts create our realities then we can choose and create our lives in more uplifting ways. Addictions to drugs and alcohol run rampant in many families spanning multiple generations. Instead of perpetuating old habits and ways of thinking caused by growing up in dysfunctional families or in bad neighborhoods, we can create positive change and break the cycle. Be the source of change and uplift your brothers and sisters. With new skills you can offer hope and healing. Rather than perpetuating dysfunction for generations to come, your new mission might include working in underserved communities to be a source of hope and healing.

Chaos and Conflict

There is so much chaos in the world, which is a reflection of our group mind fostered by fear and inner mental turmoil. When we silence our minds with meditation we become the witness or observer of our thoughts and actions. We notice the peace and the beauty within and around us. There have always been conflicts and turmoil in the world as political leaders and their followers hunger for power, control, and money. Meditation helps us to rise above conflicts and turmoil. Meditation is not escapism. Instead, it is a way to connect with people and to be fully engaged with the world while keeping our sense of self intact. For thousands of years great reformers like Christ and Buddha came to teach us to become better humans. No matter how many have shown up, the fact is, the world is still in conflict and turmoil as political and religious leaders try to hold onto power, vying for more land and resources as a result of fear and greed. When their egos get out or control, it can lead the way for dictators who harness evil energy, leading to destruction and death.

Perception

After speaking with many of the inmates, it was clear that the majority of them had grown up in families who were abusive, which may have led them to commit crimes that landed them in the slammer. Some people appear to move through life easily and are blessed with love, abundance, and success. Others have not been as fortunate and deal with despair. Our individual realities color our perceptions. I chose *Perception* as the topic of my next class, which would be beneficial for them to understand how false perception can change their individual reality. We got settled in and I asked how many of them had experiences where they misperceived something that got them into trouble. Several guys nodded their heads affirmatively. One replied, "Yes, that is exactly how I wound up here in prison. My misperception caused me to believe something that wasn't true." I explained how individuals can look at the same object or have the same experience but have very different perspectives. Based on my own experiences, I was aware that siblings who grow up in the same households with the same parents often have very different life experiences and perceptions.

The Birds

The inmates and I chatted as we exited the prison library and walked together down the sidewalk, past the metal security gate into the courtyard. The sky looked ominous as dusk began to settle into night. I looked up and witnessed thousands of black birds that filled the last bit of sunlight in the wide open spaces above. I pointed upward and shouted, "Look guys!" A paroxysm of joy surged through my being as the birds flew overhead in all different directions. There were no formations or boundaries like you might see when birds fly south for the winter. I wondered if they were honing in on food. I noticed that they were free to go in whichever direction they pleased and were not confined to any particular space or formation. I have always thought that birds are messengers of God. Native Americans believe that animals are spirit guides that show up in our lives when we need healing or support. Perhaps the birds showed up to let the inmates know that they are not alone or forgotten. I thought that the birds represented the 2,300 inmates who were incarcerated at that particular prison and appeared to offer hope, healing, and blessings. I was euphoric as the beautiful black iridescent wings spanned the wide open space of the dark blue sky as they flew haphazardly in different directions. They captured my attention as if to say, "Look at me! I am free to go whichever way I desire!" I thought about the Bible verse (Matt 6:26) where Jesus told his followers not to be anxious about food but to rely on God alone. He said, "Behold the birds in the air; they neither sow nor reap nor gather into the barns, and yet your heavenly Father feeds them." An inmate commented that he was reminded of the Alfred Hitchcock movie, *The Birds* and a few inmates laughed at that interpretation. I reminded them that this was a perfect example of how each individual interprets an object differently and how perceptions can evoke various emotions.

We separated when they were not allowed to enter the next security gate. As I continued my walk to the end of the courtyard, I passed about 100 inmates who were walking within various yellow painted lines. They had been instructed like children with coloring books to stay within the lines. The inmates call the courtyard, "the bowling alley" because they sometimes get knocked down. Some were going in the direction of the dining hall for chow while others were heading towards their dorms. I glanced at them as I walked past while trying not to draw attention to myself. I wore a bright pink blouse. A few guys who had attended my previous meditation classes recognized me and wanted to stop and talk. Others apologized for not coming to my class, especially when the guards prevented them from coming. They needed to get approval and permission to attend my class.

On one of my visits, I waited two hours in the prison diner that was designated for the guards when there were prison checks. It would not make sense to go home since I lived an hour and a half away. On rainy or bad weather days my commute could be several hours, so I preferred to wait, even when it was a long time. At times, I received an email about lockdowns or quarantines when the inmates were not allowed to leave their dorms. Sometimes guards would not allow them out when there were altercations or fights. As I passed by, several inmates got my attention. They bowed or did the Namaste prayer pose. I smiled and walked on. I observed several guards who monitored the inmates' every move while keeping them at bay. They wielded strong controlling energy. When inmates got too close to me, especially when we reached a gate simultaneously, the guards would gesture for them to stand back or stop. At times, they were reprimanded and ordered to step aside and allow me to walk through the gates first. I tried not to be overly engaged with the inmates or stop to talk to them because I didn't want to get them or myself in trouble. I needed to follow the rules if I wanted to stay in good standing with the program. I often responded with a smile, or a nod or a simple, "Bless you." I had walked with the Reverend a few times and noticed how many of the inmates stopped to talk with him. It was quite common for some of the guys to be curious about my presence at the prison. Some curious inmates would ask me what I was doing at the prison. I was not wearing a staff uniform but I was given a badge that I had to clip to my shirt or jacket to identify myself as a Chapel Volunteer. There was no way I could hide myself, even when I tried. When there were shift changes, the guards were in various stages of coming and going. I arrived at the last gate, picked up my driver's license and exited outside to the parking lot to prepare for my long commute home.

CHAPTER 9
BE AWARE AND BEWARE

I am fully aware of the unsafe prison environments, where potential danger is lurking around every corner. Even though an occasional fearful thought might pop up in my mind, I choose not to give it power by focusing on it. As the "Law of Attraction" teaches, fear will only draw more fear-provoking experiences to us.[5] When your energy vibrates at a higher level, you automatically draw to you circumstances of a similar vibration. Life becomes positive rather than negative. The frequency we're putting out with our mental broadcasting station will attract people and circumstances into our lives. If we are broadcasting fear, we are attracting the very thing we are trying to avoid. Meditation creates harmony and kindness, so when we emanate love and compassion we become a force for good. For spiritual protection, I envision an energetic shield made of white light surrounding me just like I do when walking down the streets of Chicago. It may seem strange, but when the mind can accept such a positive image, we will benefit as we rise above our fears and misconceptions. It is important to be vigilant, alert, and to pay attention to surroundings. I sense energy and observe body language of people walking or sitting nearby. Since starting my meditation program I have been asked, "Aren't you afraid to go into a maximum security men's prison?" I do not fear the guys in my class. I figure that since they are attracted to my class in the first place, their energy is conducive to learning how to find their inner source of peace, since they have a strong spiritual element within them.

While living in Chicago, I recall an evening news story that broke about a gang member in a black community on the Southside who was involved in a shootout with a rival gang member. A young mother was strolling her baby on the sidewalk when gunshots rang out. Before she could get out of harm's way, the man quickly grabbed her baby and used him as a human shield to protect himself from getting hit by gunfire. He was captured by police and wound up at the infamous Cook County Hospital in Chicago. A picture of him was splashed all over the news channels and newspapers. I wondered what kind of guy could do such a cowardly act and use an innocent baby as a human shield to protect himself?

The next day my older brother who had recent surgery was recuperating in the hospital. I was working a few blocks away and decided to pop in the hospital during my lunch hour to pay him a visit. When I walked into his room I was shocked to see the same guy whose picture was plastered all over the TV news, chained to the bed beside my brother. A police officer was sitting outside the door keeping people from the media and rival gang members at bay. The offender stared at me the entire time I was there. It felt like daggers were shooting out of his eyes. I tried to avert my vision, but needed to be vigilant in the event he figured out how to move his hospital bed closer to my brother and perhaps put him in harm's way. My brother and I chatted a little bit about his surgery and some recent events going on in our family. I briefly locked eyes with the killer and witnessed the most frightening eyes I had ever seen. Like a trapped wild animal his pitch black eyes were devoid of light and full of fear. I sensed a strong negative energy emanating from him and was concerned about my brother's wellbeing, especially if a rival gang member showed up to get revenge and use my brother as a hostage.

In retrospect, I think I needed that brief encounter to help me prepare for teaching in dangerous environments. I wondered about the life experiences of murderers that make them lose all sense of humanity. I also thought that he might have a mental disorder or perhaps had been on drugs that impaired his cognitive ability and led him to commit such a cowardly act. My high sensitivities were overwhelmed and I was beginning to feel drained. I needed to get away from his negative toxic energy. With a prayer in my heart, I kissed my brother goodbye and walked out of the room.

Changing Lives One Inmate at a Time

Knowing how important my volunteer service would be, I chose not to focus on the past or worry about the future. The past is gone and the future is not yet here. There was only the present moment so I was determined to make the best of it. I knew that lives could be changed with meditation and spiritual practices, so there was no time to waste. Being a strong advocate for justice and positive change, I was prepared to begin my humanitarian work. Teaching and bringing inmates to their inner light was possible and I was eager to help. My intent was to teach the inmates how to infuse spiritual energies in their everyday lives by using life-changing meditation and spiritual practices. Changing their lives from the inside out was the first step to advance and progress to their next levels of development and growth. Unfolding to their inner beings and spiritual natures would help not only the inmates but also others in similar situations. They might have an opportunity for an earlier parole to continue their spiritual journeys. I knew that helping the inmates on their paths to recovery and healing would not only benefit them, but would also benefit the prison environment by infusing light and positive energy.

I wanted the inmates to experience a sense of freedom by uncovering their Divine essence. Passing on powerful meditation and spiritual practices is valuable for the inmates prior to being released back into society. Based on my personal experience, I knew that if they continued doing their meditation and spiritual practices it would have a beneficial effect for the rest of their lives. Awareness is a preventative way to catch our thoughts when dealing with negative emotional states, or when faced with life challenges, Simple meditation techniques and prayer are powerful and effective ways to reduce tension that help inmates stay calm when faced with situations that assault their senses. Proper meditation programs, as taught by experienced meditation instructors, can help inmates become agents of change, thereby transforming and modifying their behaviors. Longtime meditators often report a greater sense of wellbeing. Negative emotions such as anger, anxiety, and depression dissipate at a much faster rate. Conflicts, obsessive thought patterns, and emotional triggers are diffused when we are able to observe our thoughts and actions with clarity.

I told the story of the holy man who kept committing crimes while in the presence of the police. He would throw a stone and break a window in front of a police officer knowing that he would land in jail. His disciples asked him, "Why did you do that?" The holy man replied, "There are many teachers on the outside but I need to be inside to provide teachings of love and joy." Some inmates are highly evolved and very spiritual while others are in various stages of learning. I learned that some inmates "flourish" in certain prisons and complete their undergraduate and graduate college degrees while serving time. Or they become mentors for their fellow inmates.

Throughout my decades of practicing meditation, I had learned how to tap into universal energy to align myself with strength whenever I felt vulnerable. I walked towards the chapel library where I would be teaching my next class. I passed through six or seven security gates then turned down a small wide sidewalk until I reached the chapel. I was happy to see the Chaplain waiting for me at the last gate. When I arrived inside of the building, inmates and a guard were waiting in the hallway. I presented a few fliers that I had prepared with the dates of my upcoming classes. I handed them to the Chaplain and requested that they be posted around the prison to encourage interested inmates to sign up. I suspected that some inmates signed up because they were

Doreena Durbin

curious about meditation. Others who had previous experiences with meditation were coming because they knew the value of having an opportunity to experience peace and silence, which was a rarity in the prison environment. One of the inmates, (D) was an adept of meditation and had extensive practice in a form of meditation known as Samadhi, which is the highest form of the eight limbs of yoga.

Guilt and Shame

There is no sense whatsoever in holding onto guilt and shame. One of the greatest diseases humans suffer is guilt. Shame is ego based and does not define who we are. It does no good to keep thinking about mistakes we made in our lives. Thinking about things we cannot change keeps us stuck in the past. We ruminate about what we could have done differently to prevent certain events or change the trajectories of our lives.

The past is gone and the future is not yet here. The present moment is all we have. Ruminating thoughts of how we could have acted differently keep playing like a broken record over and over in our minds. Rehashing the past, ruminating about the future, or fixating on things we cannot change creates turmoil in the body and the mind, which can ultimately be the cause of illness or disease. Healing begins when we can let them go and focus on the present moment. Why feel guilty in the present moment? Being mindful about what we are ingesting into our minds and bodies can clearly indicate where we are stuck. Mindfulness practices are useful because we are not labeling or judging. Instead, we simply acknowledge the present moment with conscious awareness.

Living in the past causes suffering for the present by stirring up old memories. The greatest gift God has given to man is the act of forgetting. How do we get rid of guilt? Analyze why you feel guilty. What makes you feel guilty? Some happening in the past causes guilt, when the past is no longer here. You must ask yourself, "Why am I feeling guilty?" But then as soon as you think of analyzing the guilt, the past reappears again on the screen of your mind.

There is a higher level of consciousness. Problems are solved by quieting your mind and asking the higher self what you need to learn from certain experiences. When you *Get An Inner Life* through the practice of meditation, you energetically raise your vibration and bring yourself in alignment with Divine energies. Then when you finally leave these iron gates and barbed wire fences behind, you will be a changed person and a better person, wiser and with more positive energy. When you experience more love and compassion, they become part of your vibration. You will begin to attract people into your life who resonate with your heightened vibration. You are learning how to think before you react and not repeat the things that you have done in the past. Paying attention to your gut reactions and knowing you are loved and accepted by our Creator will change your life.

Some people you encounter on the outside might intentionally or unintentionally ostracize you due to their fears or projections. You may have changed but they don!t know the new you. You might have to build trust. If they are sensitive to energies, they will feel that something is different about you. Or they will see more light and compassion in your eyes. With the spiritual discipline of meditation, your energy will vibrate at a higher level. People might feel your refined energy and will respond to you differently. Trust will be restored as you have become more whole and less fragmented. When you meditate regularly, you will truly be a different person. Others will see a softer, more compassionate, helpful you. They might be more willing to accept you back into the fold. Most importantly, you must accept yourself. Stop judging yourself. Let go of the past. Others will respond to you when you follow your life path with honesty and integrity—when you accept yourself as a Divine being.

Doreena Durbin

You are not learning life lessons to keep punishing yourself by repetitive thinking and remembering negative situations without the benefit of awareness. You must have the power of analysis to support your learning. The past will not be forgotten, but you can make amends by resolving the problem as much as possible. Repentance with a feeling of sincerity will help. If you robbed someone, then give back with generosity but do it in a genuine way, not for a selfish purpose. Make retribution for your past bad actions. If you injure two people with a dangerous weapon, then save two people. If you got into an auto accident and fled the scene of the crime, then stand your ground and resolve the issue before running away. Always follow your gut! If you get a nervous feeling in your solar plexus, pay attention to that feeling. You can never completely escape your crime because thoughts will continue to arise in your mind until you have the courage to face yourself with full awareness. If you lost loved ones while incarcerated and did not have the chance to say goodbye or tell them how much you love them, then tell other loved ones. Make amends by helping and serving others. They can feel your energy. If your elderly mother lives in a nursing home, go visit and share your time and light with her and others. Spend an hour or two reading a book to them, especially books with a topic that interests them. By doing that, you will bring happiness into their lives. Make someone smile. Surround yourself and others with love and light. By resolving the past, one can build a better future. You learn by your mistakes. But do not let the mistakes dominate the mind.

CHAPTER 10
RELIGION

Depending on where we were born and the families and societies in which we live, it is common to practice the religion of our families. In large cities like Chicago, people and religions are very diverse. People from all religious backgrounds are more accepted. God is omnipresent. Every cell of our bodies, no matter what religion we follow, is a manifestation of the Divine and part of the One God. We are perfect just as we are.

Individuals born in the Middle East are mostly practitioners of Islam. Inhabitants of India are mostly Hindus; there are also Sikhs, Muslims, and Christians. Throughout history, wars have been fought as a result of our religious or political differences. In order to embrace people from other religious backgrounds, tolerance and compassion are required. Judging other human beings' paths creates conflict.

Doreena Durbin

I am well aware that many people question their faith and/or condemn others. They close themselves off from learning, shutting themselves off from others around them in fear and low states of consciousness. Unfortunately, their tenacity to their way of thinking, their judgments, and their fears take precedence over the good they could be performing to heal the divisiveness we experience in politics and religion. On the worldwide scale, as a result of fear or wanting to control, and amass resources for power, these conflicts lead to wars, killing millions of people. Being a seeker of truth, I search for the similarities that tie us together rather than the differences that keep us apart. Everyone has free will to follow whichever religion resonates with their beings. Taking away their belief systems and identity can damage a person's sense of self and identity. One of the most beautiful parts of Christianity is the idea of redemption. Some are born again by the symbolic powers of baptism and salvation. I often wonder how many Christians are walking in Jesus' shadow and how many are walking in his footsteps by doing good deeds and practicing his teachings of love, compassion, and forgiveness.

In my opinion, religions should not be exclusive. Instead, they should be inclusive. Jesus accepted the saint and the sinner. Great religious leaders like Jesus did not judge or turn people away. He embraced everyone who sought truth. Any religion or no religion is also a choice. Atheism and humanism have gained popularity for those who have been disillusioned by religion. Unfortunately, many religious organizations have become very business oriented and egocentric. The fear of losing power and control over followers has been in flux for many years. The Covid pandemic changed the way many people choose to worship.

The Golden Rule is consistent in these religions:

Christianity: Do unto others as you would have them do unto you.

Islam: Not one of you truly believes until you wish for others what you wish for yourself.

Hinduism: This is the sum of duty; do not do to others what would cause pain if done to you.

Buddhism: Hurt not others in ways that you yourself would find hurtful.

Judaism: What is hateful to you, do not do to your neighbor.

Natives: Live in harmony, for we are all related. Wicca/Pagan: If it harm none, do what ye will.

During my exploration of various religions I learned that different Bibles and sacred texts are used and they all believed in One God, but there was a sense of separation. I have read a plethora of sacred religious texts. I learned that everyone has different interpretations of sacred texts, depending upon their experiences and educational backgrounds. I realized that no religion makes us superior or inferior to another. God is omnipotent and not exclusive to any one religion. That realization has provided me with a deeper understanding of religiousness and spirituality. In 1987 during the Harmonic Convergence, which was the world's first synchronized event where people gathered for a global peace meditation, I attended a Native American event in Sedona, Arizona for a Sunrise Ceremony. I participated in a sweat lodge led by a Lakota Indian tribe. It was a powerful three day event and will remain in my memory bank for the rest of my life.

"I would rather let my spirit fly free, than be caged by religion. Become a Buddha, not a Buddhist; become a Christ, not a Christian. One implies a state of awakened conscience, the other a dogmatic approach to life. "God" is too big for one religion. Love and quantum physics are my

religion. At a certain level, all religious traditions have the same purpose: to transform the individual into a positive being. I love Jesus, love Shiva, love Krishna, love Buddha. All rivers lead to the same ocean." John Lennon (singer and guitarist, The Beatles)

Belief in Reincarnation

Have you ever met someone and felt such a strong connection with them that you sensed that you knew them from another lifetime? Or that you visited somewhere and you felt like you had been before? Do you resonate with certain people and feel like an old soul? If reincarnation exists, that could explain the strong energy you feel when you come into contact with certain individuals or when you visit certain places. It's as if you have a magnetic pull (not necessarily sexual) to that person and feel like you already know details about them that you normally wouldn't know. A strong energetic pull is often felt and you keep running into that person in unusual places. Perhaps you had unfinished business with them and didn!t learn certain life lessons. Sometimes the Universe puts opportunities in our path to get it right in our current lifetimes. You attract people into your life based on your own energy field and vibration. We all learn from each other. One can only speculate what happens in the afterlife. I have heard that reincarnation is like taking off one suit and putting on another. Like bodies, when they get worn out, new bodies become available and depending upon our experiences and our karmas, the decision is made with the Creator to return as a human being to complete another life cycle. Our souls carry on. Science has shown, energy can never be destroyed or created. It just transforms. Nothing is ever destroyed. It just comes back in a different form. Every action has a reaction.

Belief in reincarnation is more accepted in India and other Asian cultures but many Native American tribes also believe in reincarnation.[6] Being so close to Mother Earth and Father Sky, they see life and nature as cyclical. They are aware of the Spirit world and the interconnectedness of all beings, ancestors, and animals. Many believe that our souls choose our parents and the circumstances in which we are born for the purpose of teaching us life lessons. The idea of reincarnation may explain karmic relationships and the issue of soul mates. However, reincarnation is not accepted by all faiths. Reincarnation has been the topic of many documentaries. Even the Greek philosopher Plato believed that the purpose of life is to correct the soul's mistakes so everyone can return back to God.

One of the biggest conventions within the Roman Empire was when Emperor Constantine invited 1800 Christian Bishops from the Catholic Church, Eastern Orthodox Church, and Oriental Orthodox Church to the city of Nicaea, which is now Iznik, Turkey. When the Council of Nicaea met in 325 AD, their purpose was to attain a consensus of the Christological issue of the Divine nature and the relationship between God the Son and God the Father. Twenty-three books were removed from the Bible if they contained controversial material, or if the early Christian leaders disagreed with them. The Gospel of St. Thomas and the Gospel of Mary were two of the non-canonical gospels. They were considered closely related to the view of the Gnostics, which was a heretic sect of Christianity in the 2nd and 3rd centuries. The Council of Nicaea squashed the belief of reincarnation. Yet Christianity supports the idea of reincarnation in the Gnostic gospel that says that John the Baptist was the reincarnation of Elijah the Prophet. In the Bible (Matt 16:13-14), Jesus asked his Disciples, "Who do people say the son of Man is?" They replied, "Some say John the Baptist, others said Elijah." This implies a belief in reincarnation, later rejected by the Christian Church. Some believe that religious leaders' intention was to control people's minds over the millennia.

Limiting Beliefs

We often get stuck in religious or political ideologies and our limited belief systems, which are often based on fear, keeping us from experiencing all there is in Oneness. In reality, there is no separation. If we are born into countries where Christianity is the predominant religion, then we tend to follow that religion. Practicing meditation can release us from fear, when we discover false misconceptions. The truth is that all religions have some form of meditation. The essence of truth is the same and is inherent in all religions. If we refuse to see the beauty and truth all around us, conflict will remain in our minds. Whichever religion we subscribe to is fine if we have a deeper understanding. If you are a Christian, including meditation will provide you with a deeper experience and understanding. Then, you will become a better Christian. If you are Muslim, meditation can help you become a better Muslim. If you are a Hindu you will become a better Hindu because you will have found some integration and a deeper experience and understanding of your religion.

The Bible tells us not to judge another. *"Judge ye not that ye be judged."* Understanding the circumstances that others have to deal with can awaken us to our own afflictions. What would we do under the same conditions and circumstances? Following in the light instead of being in the shadow will set us free. With the beautiful energies felt with meditation, we look back and see that the lessons we had to learn to become better human beings were necessary. Perhaps lessons of humility, forgiveness, or letting go of ego have to be learned? Having the right attitude in life and accepting the challenges and the circumstances we find ourselves in is a blessing. The Dalai Lama once said that if every eight year old learns to meditate, there would be no wars. Instead, peace, love, and compassion would prevail. The more people around the world meditate, the less conflict we will experience and the more compassion we will exhibit. A sense of unity and acceptance will result. Meditation and spiritual practices can literally change the world resulting in more understanding and less chaos. The common denominator for people worldwide, regardless of age, race, or socioeconomic status is the desire for peace and happiness.

There is a commonality amongst humans around suffering as many of us have experienced sadness, fear, abandonment, financial loss, and despair. Avatars have been born throughout history to offer hope and healing. They teach us how to become better humans, and to seek balance and truth to bring light and love into the world to uplift humanity. Enlightened powerful masters and deities who have come to earth, especially during times of great turmoil, have had an enormous impact on humanity. Unity Consciousness is important to bring us all together. There are also great spiritual souls who have shared their light and wisdom with humanity, such as Mahatma Gandhi, Martin Luther King, Jr., Nelson Mandela, and the 14th Dalai Lama. These powerful leaders have promoted world peace and were proponents of nonviolence. Great change results from their movement and the after effects are still felt around the world. Their enormous lights, wisdom, and pure positive energy have helped to change our world, but there is still more work to be done. Their teachings are still spreading around the world. There is only one humanity. All paths lead to God.

One Source One God

I am grateful that I had the freedom when I was growing up in a family of mostly Protestants and Catholics, to choose whichever denomination of churches and other religious institutions that I wanted to explore. That freedom led me to the understanding that there is one Creator, which includes all of humanity. To satisfy my quest for learning more about religion, I joined a Council for a Parliament of the World's Religions (CPWR) and served on the Dialogue Committee. One of the main tenets for members was not to judge or proselytize. We all had the opportunity to learn from each other. I enjoyed serving and learned a lot during the next several years by arranging and attending dialogues at Christian churches, Buddhist and Hindu temples, Zoroastrian and Muslim mosques, and Sikh gurdwaras. This was in preparation for the 1993 event to celebrate the 100th anniversary of the CPWR, which was held at the Palmer House in Chicago. The Tibetan religious and political leader the 14th Dalai Lama, who is the highest spiritual leader and head of Tibetan Buddhism, was the Keynote Speaker. At the previous world parliament in 1893, Swami Vivekananda, a Hindu monk from India and leader of the Vedanta movement, was the keynote speaker. He was responsible for bringing Eastern religion to the Western world. I sponsored a Tibetan immigrant in 1991 to come to America, and was invited to a gathering at the Palmer House to meet the Dalai Lama. He wanted to thank us for our service. I was allowed to bring my children for the opportunity to meet this great leader. One of the Tibetan monks gestured for me to sit near them in the front row. They remembered me when I visited their monastery in Madison, Wisconsin with a Buddhist monk from Thailand who was responsible for inviting me to join the Dialogue Committee for CPWR. At one of our monthly meetings, he gave me the nickname, "The Bridge" because of my ability to connect people from various religions. The Dalai Lama's smiling face and warm spirit touched me deeply as I stood next to him. We greeted each other with, "Tashi Delek," the Tibetan greeting, which means, "May all good things come to you."

In an effort to understand the diverse Christian faith, I explored many denominations, including Baptist, Methodist, Lutheran, Nazarene, Greek Orthodox, Roman Catholic, Unitarian, and many others. Most recently, I explored the Jehovah Witness and Mormon faiths. I tuned into their similarities rather than their differences. I learnt that all religions believed in the same God. They just had different prophets, beliefs, dogmas, and creeds. There is no question that Jesus made a great impact and spread his teachings around the world, which continues today. Many people consider their religion to be the one and only true religion. They were only told to believe. Throughout history religious leaders often used fear as a means of controlling their flock. People who think differently are a threat to them. They do not understand nor do they have the courage of their own convictions to step outside of their comfort zones to allow open dialogues. What a rich world we would live in if we could do that with acceptance and without judgment!

Meditation promotes peace and understanding amongst all people. The Bible tells us to meditate. Nearly every religion has some form of meditation. According to James Finley (*Christian Meditation, Experiencing the Presence of God*), Christians have practiced meditation as a way of experiencing and responding to God's presence in their daily lives.[7] Jesus, the 14th Dalai Lama, Martin Luther King, and many other religious leaders have taught loving kindness, non violence, and service to humanity. Sadly some of Jesus' teachings have been inaccurately interpreted causing hatred, anger, or revenge. Did Jesus grab a weapon to get revenge for how he was mistreated? No! He did not! He was a great example of love and compassion. The majority of people living in America are Christians. But how many Christians really live Jesus's teachings? Are they following in Jesus's shadow or in Jesus's light? When they follow in his shadow, they may be able to quote scriptures or pray in a rote manner; however, are they practicing what they preach? When they live in Jesus' light, they are doing good deeds, treating others with love, respect, and kindness, and are not judging others because they think differently.

Most prayers serve the same purpose, which is to connect with and communicate with God. While serving on CPWR, I had the opportunity to attend religious ceremonies representing nearly all of the world religions. I observed people getting blessed by a priest or swami in the Catholic and Hindu faiths. As they were blessed with water, ashes, or kumkum paste (used for religious markings centered in the forehead) people were not focusing on the spiritual aspects and meaning of the spiritual blessings they were receiving. Instead, they were distracted by talking with each other while in line to receive those sacred blessings, and not focused on the prayers invoked on their behalf. They were not focusing on the present moment. I wondered how many people

Doreena Durbin

really understood the Communion practice that is done in Catholic or Lutheran churches? I wonder if they feel the powerful words that are invoked when their minds and attention are wandering all over the place?

CHAPTER 11

THE HISTORY OF MEDITATION

Meditation is believed to have started in India thousands of years ago. Today there are many different traditions, which have been adopted by other religions in various countries around the world. The Upanishads is considered to have the earliest written records about meditation. These sacred, philosophical texts were written in Sanskrit c. 800-200 BC. The main idea of the Upanishads is that everything in the Universe is interconnected and has a unifying principle in the cosmos. God is One.

Perhaps a state of meditation was achieved unconsciously by observing an outside fire used for warmth or cooking or being in the midst of nature, but eventually it was done consciously with intention. Enlightened spiritual teachers (gurus) who had learned these ancient techniques, offered instruction and guidance on how to access our own inner gurus so we could experience the Kingdom of God within.

What is Meditation?

Meditation is a heightened state of awareness where we connect with our inner selves. As we turn our attention from the outer world to the rich inner world to allow our real selves to experience the peace and silence that is inherent within us, we will naturally

Doreena Durbin

elevate to a higher state of consciousness and awareness. A qualified meditation teacher is trained to lead you systematically, step-by-step through the conscious level of the mind to the subconscious level, until you reach the superconscious level of the mind where the source of all knowledge resides. You are taught to use a focal point like the breath, a mantra, or a visual object as you begin from the conscious level of the mind, to the subconscious level, where impressions and memories are stored, until you reach the superconscious level where you draw upon Divine energies.

Meditation is different from the sleep or the waking state where there is metacognition or awareness and understanding of one's own thought processes. Sleep produces delta waves while beta waves are evident when working on tasks and problem solving. Electrical activity occurs in the brain whether you are mentally active, resting, or sleeping, which suggests that even during meditation or deep relaxation, the mind is not void of thoughts. Thoughts, memories, and images emerge from the subconscious mind. During meditation, you simply allow thoughts to come and go effortlessly without controlling them in any way. The goal is to go beyond the mind to the peace and silence that resides within. The mind and thoughts are the biggest obstacles to experiencing peace. The mind has a mind of its own. It is difficult to rein it in. Letting go of thoughts and bringing your attention back to your breathing or a mantra is a simple way to bring yourself into alignment with your inner self. Like monkeys jumping from tree to tree, the mind will jump from one thought to another. Some people get frustrated because they have the false impression that the mind is supposed to be blank during the meditative state. Nothing could be further from the truth! Try it...you'll see. In my class, the inmates learn how to deal with the phenomenon of an overactive mind and how to go beyond thoughts.

Another practice involves the power of visualization where you focus on a visual object, like a candle flame. It stimulates

74

the Ajna chakra whose physiological counterpart is the pineal gland, which secretes melatonin and induces sleep. Putting your attention on the third eye increases intuitive faculties, insight, and our connection with the spiritual realm. It has been practiced for thousand of years and can release stress and tension.

Bringing one's attention to a focal point is a good exercise for our scattered minds. When the power of attention and concentration is increased, one-pointedness also increases making the mind feel like a laser beam. We unfold to our inherent intuition and pay more attention to our gut feelings. Having a focused mind can make the difference between success and failure. Therefore, this spiritual practice can help one overcome a scattered mind and provide balance.

Many books describe various practices but having intellectual or book knowledge without actual experience is useless. There is no comparison to a live teacher. Some teachers emanate a spiritual force that is felt by the student. However, it is important to know that the spiritual force does not come from the teacher or healer. The teacher only acts as a channel, aligned with universal energy, which flows naturally. Once spiritual disciplines are practiced with regularity, the meditator will notice differences within himself or herself when tapping into their inner beings. During the meditative state, when dealing with noise and distractions, it is important that when sounds enter into conscious awareness we treat them as thoughts because they will generate thoughts. Allow them to become part of the experience, let them go, then return back to the breath or mantra.

The importance of regularity cannot be underestimated. Like a glass of dirty water that is put under a dripping faucet, the water gets cleaner and more purified with each clean drop. The more you meditate, the more purified your mind and body will become as they are detoxified. It seems as if humans remember negative experiences more than positive experiences. Brain

75

activity focusing on negative thoughts keeps playing over and over in our minds and prevents us from experiencing tranquility and joy. When negative, fearful thoughts are allowed to continue for extended periods of time, illness and disease can manifest. Thinking about how we could have done things differently is not going to change the outcome. Negative ruminating thoughts not only keep us stuck but they can also prevent us from living in the present moment. It does no good whatsoever to continue beating ourselves up for misdeeds we have made while not being consciously aware of the consequences of our actions. Each time a meditator focuses on the breath or a mantra, he or she digs down deeper and deeper within themselves shining light on the darkness, which activates a spiritual force. Hope replaces despair, discord becomes harmonious, and love replaces hate. Some report that after experiencing the permanent highs from meditation, their attachments and cravings are lessened.

What is the Purpose of Meditation?

The purpose of meditation is to integrate and harmonize the body, mind, and spirit. When you reach the silence within, you only need a glimpse to feel the power of this ancient technique as you lead the mind deep within yourself, where the vast reservoir of energy resides. You draw upon that energy whenever you feel disconnected. When you draw upon that energy the patterning of the subconscious mind changes, which helps you become calmer and more peaceful. As you learn to observe your thoughts or feelings without judgment, then you will find it is easier to let go of attachments to outcomes in the waking state. Our lives take on beautiful hues where more light and positive energy permeate our bodies and minds, thereby lessening the effects of stress, illness, and disease. With regular practice of meditation, a noticeable change is felt in the body and mind. The mind feels lighter and unencumbered and the body feels more relaxed. Things that used to bother you no longer affect you because you will see things from a different perspective. We acknowledge the part we play in reacting negatively when altercations arise that trigger our emotions. When love replaces hatred, hope replaces despair, light replaces darkness, and pardon replaces offense then we are free to be who we really are without judgments. A sense of lightness and joy is felt resulting in a feeling of compassion, understanding, and empathy towards other sentient beings. We disempower ourselves when we allow others to control our moods and dispositions. Through meditation we realize that their judgments of us become their problems, not ours. We can learn to observe our emotions by silently invoking the mantra or by engaging the breathing practice. Once we embrace who we really are, relationships can heal easier. Our attitudes and reactions change when we take back our power. When inmates are spiritually awakened, their entire being changes. In time, when more inmates get involved in spiritual practices, the energy field in the prison is infused with positivity and inmates are uplifted. The energy in the prison becomes lighter, allowing love, joy, and compassion to permeate the harsh environment. Inmates find that they are naturally drawn to peace and seek out more opportunities to experience the silence within.

During the meditative state we tune into our inner beings or higher selves by staying in the present moment, by not allowing our attention to wander. Learning tools that break through the darkness into our inner selves and connecting to the infinite Universe might be a bit scary for some. Know that we are part and parcel of everything and everyone around us, and know that we can never step into the same river twice because it keeps changing and changing. Paying attention to the negative thoughts we harbor will only keep us stuck into never ending cycles of pain and grief. During meditation we are learning how to let go of thoughts while returning to a focal point. This method has been practiced by spiritual adepts for eons. We must learn about the purpose of life and how to rise above pettiness. It does not replace religion. Instead, it enhances religions with new, more insightful understanding. The difference between knowledge and wisdom is that knowledge is about acquiring facts about a subject such as science or history. Wisdom is experiential and comes from learning from our mistakes and not repeating them. Wisdom is more profound and comes from a level of knowingness where you are aligned with the truth. Uncovering inner wisdom is one of the most important benefits of meditation. Life changing truths can bring new energy into our thoughts and actions so that more will light can shine through. When they are tense or negative, the body feels a sense of heaviness. When we uplift our vibrations and infuse finer and finer energy into every cell of our bodies, our vibrations become lighter and we emanate more light and positivity. Then we unfold to inner peace and happiness. Acceptance is key to tolerating certain life situations and conditions.

When coming out of the meditative state one feels more calm and exhibits a gentler disposition. The Kingdom of Heaven within offers peace and tranquility. That peace permeates your thoughts and actions. You have a greater ability to accept life as it is.

Divinity has given us the gifts of grace and mercy. There is a sense that everything in your life is exactly how it should be. The ability to face challenges becomes easier, especially with the power of grace. The more we accept our current reality and the more awareness we have, the easier it is to find the opportunity or blessing that is inherent within adversities. We find it easier to keep our egos in check and not to react in states of unawareness. Compassion, kindness, and forgiveness of ourselves and others is necessary to eradicate our negative thoughts or misdeeds. Because of our connection with other sentient beings, we find that whatever we do to others, we do to ourselves.

Science on the Molecular Level

While walking outside of my class one of the inmates suggested that I speak more about science. He said since men use more of the logical left side of their brain, they are more interested in the science of meditation, so this section is in honor of those men.

Meditation has been shown to heal the body on the molecular level.

Everything in our Universe is made up of energy vibrating at different frequencies. Our thoughts are also energy as well as plants, animals, and rocks. As we tune to higher frequencies, the atmosphere around us changes. Meditation is a way to elevate our consciousness. Our ability to perceive is heightened as we align with universal energies. Perception, cognition, and unconditional love are some of the properties of having a heightened state of self awareness.

The Brain on Meditation

There are billions of cells in the brain. Meditation helps to balance the left hemisphere and right hemisphere of the brain. We each have a defense system that when activated, increases T-cells and antibodies, which keep our immune systems strong to fight off viruses and bacteria. Meditation acts like a light switch in the brain. Some of the benefits include less stress, better memory, deeper and better sleep, and more happiness. Longterm meditators have an ability to recover quickly from stressful situations. Just 10 minutes a day of meditation can increase the alpha (relaxation) waves and decrease anxiety and depression. Our bodies have about 50 trillion living cells. When they harmonize with each other, our bodies are healthy. When disharmony occurs, then disease is likely to manifest.

Brain waves change with meditation. The longer you have been practicing, the more benefits you receive. Meditators report they are calmer and more aware. They have a better sense of wellbeing and they can catch themselves much quicker before making a mistake or reacting without awareness. In the meditative state there is a systematic process that brings us from the outer world to the inner world where stillness resides.

Emotional triggers and adrenaline will surge through the body when there is a threat. Witnessing the bodily effects of the fight or flight syndrome is necessary for humans, just as it is for all members of the animal kingdom. Homeostasis and balance can be restored much quicker with the valuable tools of mindfulness and breathing exercises.

The Benefits of Meditation

Do the body and mind change with meditation? Absolutely! The body doesn't age as rapidly. Meditators often exhibit a beautiful glow on their faces in the form of love and compassion. The more like-minded people and meditators we surround ourselves with, the more accepted and uplifted we feel as more love and light filters through. Many people suffer depression and think that they are unloved. However, it is only when they become aware of their own goodness and start loving themselves that they can feel the love and see the light in others. Then they will attract love and kindness from others. Become lovable, and you will attract love. People are drawn to lovable spirits. Self pity and wallowing in negative depressive thoughts backed up with anxieties and feelings of guilt are not conducive to our spirits. When we incorporate spiritual practices into our lives, we are uplifted and will attract more happiness.

There are many challenges in life: working, financial issues, overwhelming responsibilities taking care of our families, and dealing with difficult relationships. Stress builds up for years until one day we wake up from sleep walking and decide to change our lives for the better. During challenges, depression may occur and we might be tempted to fall back into self made traps of negative thinking and old habits. We try to cover up the pain sometimes looking for temporary relief. Falling into self induced traps creates a negative aura around us, which sets up a vicious cycle of wanting more and more to ease the emotional or physical pain. Drug addicts frequently lose their jobs, a place to live, and relationships. Give yourself an opportunity to live a better life filled with love and joy.

Having a regimen of meditation can relieve PTSD. Opening the heart allows more love, compassion, and empathy to permeate. When faced with situations that assault our senses, a regular regimen of meditation and prayer is beneficial. It has a positive impact on the inmate as well as people around him. It is also beneficial for emotional regulation and non-judgmental awareness, which can result in a reduction of criminal behavior.

Studies have shown that practicing meditation for at least 20 minutes per day, preferably twice a day can:

- enhance a sense of wellbeing,
- promote a sense of peace and calm,
- decrease anger and irritability,
- reduce fears and anxiety,
- control panic attacks,
- improve self esteem.

CHAPTER 12
ATTACHMENTS

Buddhists have very simple teachings. They say that impermanence is like a flowing river. You can never step into the same river twice. Life is constantly changing. In reality, the only constant is change. Swimming *with* the current instead of against it makes life easier. Imprisonment can feel like an eternity while life is going on around us. Attachments to the way things used to be or how they should be emerge in our minds and cause suffering. Meditation teaches us to let go of things we cannot control or cannot change. Everything around us is composed of energy all vibrating at different frequencies. Words and sounds also carry energy, vibrations, and power. Saying, "I am Divine," instead of saying "I am a sinner," will have a life changing effect on your state of mind. Changing your way of thinking from a negative viewpoint to more positivity can do wonders for your body and mental wellbeing. If you keep saying, "I am sick," you will become sicker. This can apply to anything we repeat over and over in our minds. If someone has told you repetitively that you are a bad person and have no value, you do not have to accept their negative thoughts. You have changed. Other people's projections and opinions about you are their business, not yours. They may be holding you in a place you were in the past. When they begin to see the positive changes in you, only then can they give up their old perceptions. Our deeds do not define who we really are. As you make progress in your spiritual practices, more light can shine through replacing the darkness.

Healing Begins Within

All people need love and support. Every human being is connected with Source energy but we also need human love, understanding, and acceptance. We just have to realize it by uncovering the veils of ignorance that keep us from knowing the truth about ourselves. When we realize that we are and have always been part of the whole and connected with Source energy, we will notice improvement in our lives. We become more conscious of our thoughts and actions that keep us stuck on hamster wheels going nowhere. Staying present is the key to ending misery and suffering. One of the life lessons involved with growing spiritually is learning to embrace our strengths as well as our weaknesses with understanding and non-judgment. Life is a school. We are all here to learn how to become better human beings, helping ourselves and humanity. At the end of our lives, we think about our mistakes and wish we could have been more loving, and had treated others with more kindness, or had an opportunity to go back and spend quality time with them. It takes courage to heal relationships so it is important to deal with them while we are embodied.

In 1994, I recall sitting next to my 37 year old friend in a Chicago hospital. He was on his death bed. Even in his young age, he had wisdom and a soul of a saint. He knew he didn't have much time. We often regret that we did not tell our loved ones how much we love them. We wish we could go back say the right things or share ourselves with them selflessly and without ego. I sat by his bedside and asked, "Steve, if you could do it all over again is there anything you would change or do differently?" He said, "Yes, take time to smell the roses. If I could do it all over again I would have spent more time with my loved ones and less time at work." The importance of healing relationships can never be overestimated. Carrying those memories and hurt and pain into other relationships will continue until we learn how to be more loving, forgiving, and compassionate. We must free ourselves from suffering and regrets while we have the opportunity...while

Doreena Durbin

we are still alive. Having the courage to look at ourselves squarely in the face is difficult, but forgiveness for ourselves and others is an important step in healing emotional wounds. It may be difficult, but it is well worth the effort. Courage is needed to face our inner demons and to forgive others. A sense of freedom is experienced as we release our emotional burdens.

CHAPTER 13
HEART CONNECTION

I love the diversity of people coming together in my classes. We have a heart connection with each other. No one fights or disagrees with each other. We are here to learn, not to judge. We respect each other's views and opinions. By understanding each other and allowing others to be who they are, I believe hatred and discord are lessened. Perhaps people on the outside should learn some lessons from people on the inside. Some people have contempt for anyone who doesn't fit into their ideological boxes. We cut ourselves off from learning because of our limited viewpoint. Sometimes we block ourselves from experiencing new ideas and concepts, which could allow our lives to become fuller and richer. Normal Vincent Peale said, "The way to happiness: Keep your heart free from hate, your mind from worry. Live simply, expect little, give much." The power of positive thinking can only go so far. When you align yourself with the vastness of the Universe, new thoughts will be generated and you will attract wellness.

The inmates in my class span several generations, races, and religious backgrounds. We energetically pass information back and forth during the teaching/learning process. I feel a sense of commonality as love and compassion expand from my inner being to theirs, no matter our differences in gender and age. I see them as brothers, cousins, or sons. At times, I almost forget that it is taboo to have physical contact and have to refrain from hugging them or patting them on the back. Perhaps they made some bad decisions but now they are here to rectify and redeem themselves by serving time. Some of them are attracted to my class because they want to grow spiritually and to experience freedom through the process of meditation. Some are just curious while others are spiritual adepts, and flow. When my heart connects with their hearts, I feel the Divinity that resides within them. I want them to know that as children of God, they are valued and worthy. As we walk together down the courtyard, I feel like they are my posse. I feel a strong sense of protection and connectedness. I am happy to share their space and time.

Prayers and Chants

Invoking sacred prayers or certain chants that are a part of various religious and spiritual practices is vibrationally uplifting. They stimulate both hemispheres of the brain and have a calming effect on the nervous system. When people come together for healing, chants, and prayer, an energetic alignment with the group is experienced when all members are chanting or in harmony. We resonate with each other to create a powerful vibration that accelerates healing. After chanting, deeper meditations result.

CHAPTER 14

THE PURSUIT OF HAPPINESS

The birthright of all human beings is to be happy. Be yourself. However, if we only see our imperfections and are self critical, we will have difficulty seeing our perfection. Trying to be someone else is not conducive to our beings. Self integration is a gift that we share for ourselves and people around us. Walking into a room filled with people who are thinking thoughts of gloom and doom, sensitive beings can pick up that negative energy. Energetically, you might not feel comfortable standing or sitting close to negative people, and you will try to avoid being in their presence. On the other hand, if you are feeling a sense of love, joy, and peace, others will be attracted to your beautiful energy and will want to be in your beautiful presence. Then when you walk into a room others will be drawn to you because that energy will be emitted without your having to say a word. Animals are also drawn to positive energy. It is recommended that you do not allow cats and dogs to sit on your lap when you are meditating because they feel your peaceful energy and want to be a part of it. They can also be a source of distraction. It is best to build up your own energy; then you can share it with them afterwards and it will be more beneficial for you and them.

Finding pleasure in the present moment is the goal in life. We seek outside of ourselves thinking that we will find happiness by

Doreena Durbin

going on vacations, to movies, and other forms of entertainment. Sooner or later, we discover that no matter how much money or possessions we have acquired, searching outside of ourselves will not bring us joy. Simple ways of being in the now are spending time in nature, listening to music, meditating, or praying. Make your garden beautiful by tending to your spirit. Mind is full of conflicts but with self integration of the body, mind, and spirit, we can function in harmony. Then there is no conflict and life becomes tranquil. Everything is eternal and immortal. Evolution continues to move us forward. When we are integrated, free will merges into Divine will.

Living in the present moment is difficult when the mind is fragmented. Integration and oneness are the keys to finding peace. Most of us live in the past. Our minds are filled with all kinds of memories, but most people tend to fixate on negative memories. Good or bad deeds fill our minds and we project our memories into the future. When we put so much attention on the future, we tend to miss the present moment. By focusing on the breath or a mantra the ability to go deeper into the meditative state occurs and we tap into the subconscious mind where impressions and memories are stored. Starting with the conscious level of the mind with a focus on the breath or a mantra, one can systematically reach the superconscious level of the mind where you draw upon Divine energies. When our subconscious minds as well as our mental and physical bodies become integrated, stress is released and we become tranquil. Once good energy and peace permeate your thoughts and daily actions, you can share those positive energies with others around you. When meditation is utilized in prisons, the inmates are more calm and a ripple effect of pure positive energy is felt and spreads from one inmate to another.

Life can be heaven or hell. We either focus on fear or we focus on love. Either way, it is *our* choice based on our free will. Life itself can feel like a prison when you are dealing with stress. We strive to overcome challenges but they often keep repeating. We create our own prisons in our minds. Years of building walls to protect ourselves from the onslaughts and conflicts of people around us can be very damaging. Look for the best in your current circumstances. Everyone has an opportunity for greatness. It just needs to be uncovered. You can be a source of good and uplift your fellow man, or you can be a source of pain and spread negativity wherever you go. It is entirely up to you. Make the best of your time in prison, away from society. When you wake up to a whole new day, have hope for a better day and a better future. Have more fellowship with the other inmates. Humanity's purpose is to serve, so we must make the best of it. Be grateful that you are given another day to live and to become a better more loving person.

"Every day, think as you wake up, today I am fortunate to be alive, I have a precious human life, I am not going to waste it. I am going to use all my energies to develop myself, to expand my heart out to others, to achieve enlightenment for the benefit of all beings. I am going to have kind thoughts towards others, I am not going to get angry or think badly about others. I am going to benefit others as much as I can." 14th Dalai Lama

Meditation will do wonders for your well-being as positive energies and vibrations are infused. Starting your day with a nice meditation will set the tone. Use compassion with your brothers in prison as well as for yourself. You will notice your life becomes more tolerable and even joyful when you are in a higher vibration. Look for the pearl inherent in the oyster of your current situation. Be grateful that you have a place to sleep, food to eat, programs for uplifting your soul, and a few moments of peace. Having the proper perspective will show you that there is freedom in bondage when you stop projecting yourself into the future and learn to live here now in the present moment. Many of us are victims of circumstances. Being locked up in prison where we have no direct responsibilities for taking care of our households or paying our debts can be perceived by some as a blessing.

Doreena Durbin

The common denominator for humans worldwide is a desire for happiness and freedom. Hatred is a low vibration energy. Blaming others for things they cannot control like being born in certain races or groups will keep us stuck in lower vibrations and frequencies. Hatred of the other keeps us stuck in negative patterns and lowers our vibrations. This includes hatred of others who may be from certain political affiliations, which promotes violence and conflict. When we resonate with higher frequencies, we raise our vibrations and can easily accept all of our Creator's sentient beings. The Biblical injunction of "Loving your neighbor as thyself" cannot be done unless you have awareness in the recognition that everything around you is no different from yourself. The essence of everything is One. We are not separate from each other. There is one continuum. Our minds are fragmented, therefore we see separation. Seek balance. The goal is to be integrated to find balance. Once you unfold to that awareness, life becomes an amazing canvas to create whatever you desire. We are co-creators with the Universe.

Drugs and Alcohol

Many people are trapped within their own minds and try to cover up fear and anger. Some turn to drugs and alcohol when dealing with emotional pain and suffering. The highs and lows that we get from drugs and alcohol are temporary and will not bring permanent relief from suffering. As soon as the effects wear off, we feel miserable again. We want to tap into the source of happiness and peace to a more permanent state of being. An excessive amount of drugs and alcohol stagnates our spiritual growth. Our bodies will suffer, especially if we are sensitive to these substances. Some lessons are very difficult to learn but are necessary for our soul's development. Being mindful about the effect drugs have on us will keep us safe from harm and may also keep us out of prison. Some of our lessons are deeply rooted, especially when we suffer emotional wounds, which can cause illness and disease.

90

Compassion, empathy, and understanding can do wonders for emotional wellbeing. Loving kindness is essential in healing ourselves and others. Many inmates grew up in drug and/or alcohol infested homes, where one or both parents are offenders. Good role models are important for children who were born into families where one or both parents were unavailable as a result of divorce, separation, or incarceration. Until social organizations determine that children are in need of support, it is often too late to undo the damage that has been done, especially on the emotional level. Children and families often suffer the consequences. For some people, challenges and disadvantages can awaken them and put them on a different trajectory of life. Being committed to serve time in prison can be a very harsh lesson but it can also be a blessing, which may take years to realize. Like energy, our spirits can never be created nor destroyed. Nothing can ever break our spirits because we are manifestations of the infinite Universe. Once we become integrated, negativity dissipates.

If you have done something wrong like robbing a store or have been violent with someone, there is nothing you can do to undo the damage that has been done. It does no good whatsoever to ruminate about your wrongdoings unless there is a plan to learn from the past. Keeping those thoughts alive and reliving them will not help anyone but instead will keep you stuck in a never ending cycle of guilt and shame. You cannot force yourself to have positive thoughts but you can bring integration to your mind by infusing meditation and spiritual practices. Then negativity vanishes and thoughts of revenge dissipate.

Synthesizing Science and Spirituality

Neurogenesis occurs with the development of nerve tissues. Just like the body that sits or sleeps all day long the brain is the same... use it or lose it. The brain generates new neurons when working on crossword puzzles, playing musical instruments, doing math or creative arts. Right brained activity increases the brain's ability to reinvent itself. Meditation stimulates the brain. The brain benefits from meditation and increases neurons. It boosts serotonin also known as the "happy" neurotransmitter, and other good chemicals. Stress leads to depression and low serotonin levels. New brain cells increase happiness. Stress increases the hormones of cortisol and adrenaline, which destroys healthy muscle and bone. Researchers at UC Davis in 2013 found a correlation between mindfulness and cortisol. A 50% reduction of cortisol levels was discovered within just a few short weeks of daily meditation. In a study from Rutgers University, there was a 50% reduction of cortisol levels in meditators, which was beneficial for stress relief.[7] Meditation controls anxiety through the mind-body connection. It slows metabolism, reduces heart rate, slows aging, boosts endorphins and melatonin.

Mental benefits include: neurogenesis, quiet mind chatter, increased intuition and awareness of the fight or flight responses. This is our built in street defense mechanism (parasympathetic nervous system) that reacts to perceived threats of survival. Thinking pain creates more pain. When you are in the dental chair or in a medical situation, when you focus on the breath, your anxiety will lessen and the pain will subside because you're putting your attention elsewhere by not focusing on the pain.

Physical benefits include: strengthened immunity, gut health, and the "butterfly feeling" in the solar plexus associated with nervous tension. It is a warning sign that something is wrong.

A Prison Meditation Program was introduced to inmates at San Quentin and Folsom prisons in California in the 1970s. Meditation is truly transformational as a way to help prisoners deal with aggressive behavior. In the 1960s the practice was researched extensively at Harvard by Dr. Herbert Benson, *Relaxation Response*, who was studying health benefits.[8]

Activating prana (life force) is one of the best ways to calm down quickly when faced with negative situations that trigger our emotions. When biochemicals of emotions are released in our bodies, it causes the fight and flight response, which is a physiological reaction to stress due to a threat of survival. This is a defense mechanism which is crucial for all animals and is very positive in life threatening situations. Heart palpitations, sweating, dilated pupils, and increased blood flow to the muscles are some of the bodily sensations that occur when an adrenaline rush is activated. This can happen even when stopped for a traffic violation or an auto accident due to fear of the police, especially when carrying drugs or weapons. Using the 4:16:8 (breathing in on the count of 4, holding your breath for a count of 16 and exhaling on the count of 8) exercise is crucial for quickly calming down the body and mind when provoked. Being mindful and aware of the triggers can de-escalate raging emotions of anger or fear. Having breathing tools can make the difference in spending additional time in jail or prison because of being provoked and reacting without awareness. Serving a longer sentence or spending time in solitary confinement can be avoided when using spiritual practices and meditative tools.

I recall when my son started driving at age 16. He came home and told me he was stopped by the police for speeding. As he shared the incident with me I noticed that his face and eyes were filled with anger. I asked him if he spoke to the Officer the same way as he was when sharing the incident with me. I told him that if I was the Officer, and he had the same angry, defensive look on his face, I would have given him a ticket too. I told him that the next time he gets stopped by the police to calm down by taking a deep breath, smile and say...Good afternoon Officer, then do your best to speak in a calm voice. Several months later, he came home and said, Mom, it worked! I got stopped by the police, followed your advice and said,"Good morning." The police officer reacted differently and did not give him a citation. Acting defensively and angrily will only escalate the situation. When you get the first signs of an adrenaline rush and want to run or fight, that's the time to prepare yourself and change your energies from negative to positive by taking a deep breath. Learning the 4:16:8 breathing technique is a powerful way to calm down quickly.

I completely understand that the last thing you would want is to be sent to jail so your situation might not be so easy as it was for my son. Especially since you may already have previous convictions or incarcerations and have horrible memories and being stopped and detained. Becoming a repeat offender and being sent back to prison can be very frightening and many would try to avoid it at all costs.

The benefit of increased awareness is a valuable tool for staying out of prison. It is also beneficial for tolerating prison life. Becoming aware of thoughts and emotions that trigger emotional outbursts is important for the wellbeing of the inmates, guards, and the prison at large. Having fewer incidents of violence benefits the inmates and uplifts the vibrations in the prison. Having the ability to observe thoughts and recognize subtle nuances that occur in the body before reacting impulsively is a powerful internal mechanism for reducing stress.

The Law of Opposites is a paradox. We appreciate light when we are surrounded by darkness. We appreciate good health after we recover from an illness. In order to fully understand peace we must experience chaos. We co-create with the Universe to work out our soul contracts as we participate in the grand design of the Universe.

Duality exists in our world. Negative and positive, love and hate, dark and light, hard and soft, good and evil, happiness and sadness, male and female. Positive thoughts will bring positive results, whereas negative thoughts will manifest the opposite and bring negative results. Thought formations consist of energy. We can manifest good results by invoking prayer, affirmations, or by simply meditating. The human mind has enormous potential. We can shape our own reality with the power of intention and consciousness. The Universe pervades what is out there but it is also deeply interwoven within the energetic patterns of our emotions, thoughts, and intentions. Spiritual practices strongly benefit us by changing our lives for the better to attract people and situations that resonate with our inner beings.

Law of Attraction is basically...Like attracts like. Whatever frequency you are sending out; you get back. What you think or what vibration and frequency you resonate with will be returned to you. The *Law of Attraction* says that whatever we emanate we attract.

We draw people, jobs, or relationships that resonate with our beings. We are more powerful than we think. It is your thoughts and actions that bring about the corresponding reaction.

At our core, we all have a Divine connection to all that is. Like drops in the ocean, we are part of the same ocean. The *Law of Attraction* draws to you circumstances to a similar vibration based on the thoughts you are emitting. Imagine that the circumstances are already in your experience. The *Law of Attraction* basically means that we attract according to our thoughts. Positive thoughts bring positive results, whereas negative thoughts bring negative results. We attract wealth, relationships, success, and happiness based on what we are. We radiate energy and when we find a vibrational match to what we are, manifestation will naturally occur. Our thoughts and emotions create vibrational frequencies. Negative emotions like anxiety and fear will bring us exactly what we think. We cannot attract wealth when we constantly think of ourselves as being poor. Stop saying to yourself, "I'm so poor." We are co-creators with the Universe. We cannot send mixed signals or incoherent intentions or desires to the Universe if we are truly sincere about manifesting a new reality. We must generate positive, clear thoughts to get what we want. Whatever vibration and frequency we align with, the Universe responds to the electric charge of our thoughts and boomerangs, providing us with synchronicity, which is our sign that the Universe is responding to our requests.

If your heart is filled with love, love is returned tenfold. And that is an indisputable law. Because of the heightened awareness, your heart opens and unfolds with love so you have good, positive thoughts, and you become lovable as you dive deeper and deeper within yourself. You discover that you are beautiful just as you are. Then you see the beauty in everything around you. Love is needed to heal ourselves, our loved ones, and humanity. Without love, we feel lost, lonely, and abandoned. These emotions can set up depressive thoughts that lead to full blown depression.

CHAPTER 15

INCARCERATION

Homelessness, sexual abuse, domestic violence, addictions, and witnessing or being involved in crimes have a deep impact on the human psyche. Both the perpetrator and the victim find it difficult to heal from traumatic episodes, which manifest as uncontrolled anger, fear, anxiety, nightmares, and PTSD. Feelings of guilt, shame, and blame create patterns of emotion that are rooted in the subconscious mind and are triggered by outside events. Is there hope for inmates in prison? Yes, there is. Offering positive resources such as prison ministry, and meditation and mindfulness programs can free prisoners from being locked up in the body and mind, thereby giving them a new lease on life. Resources that promote positive understanding and learning opportunities can have life changing effects on inmates, and also create better functioning prison systems that encourage peace over hostility and violence.

It comes as no surprise that the majority of inmates have grown up in dysfunctional home environments where support and resources were lacking. Poverty, drugs, alcohol, depressions and other mental health issues are the primary reasons for the problems in families and communities. Children in many households are being raised by a single parent. One or both parents may be serving time in prison. Fear and anxiety dominate their lives. When inmates find themselves locked up for crimes, trauma continues. The negative attitudes inmates portray towards authority figures often

Doreena Durbin

manifest as anger and aggression. They sometimes have difficulty accepting responsibility for their actions, which may cause them to be insensitive to the impact of their criminal behavior, especially if they are sociopaths. They ruminate about what they could have done differently to prevent an incident from happening in the first place. They feel despair and powerlessness over things they cannot change or control. Unable to change the past, they seek ways to control the present and change future possibilities. Replacing hatred and anger with empathy, compassion, and forgiveness are the first steps in changing someone's behavior to improve the prison environment.

Victims and Low Vibration Energy

Some people who are serving time are sitting in jail for crimes they didn't commit because they cannot make bail. Lots of people are affected when a loved one is imprisoned. Family members often suffer from their absence. Some of the incarcerated "victims" are stuck in the penal system for decades. DNA specimens can be instrumental in proving the innocence of these unfortunate inmates. At the same time, there are also prisoners serving time who committed heinous crimes and deserve incarceration in order to protect innocent people in society. There is no doubt that these criminals need to be taken off the streets because they are a threat to society. Gun laws are lax in many states in the U.S., especially when involving assault weapons, which are readily available and can kill innocent victims at a high rate. Fear has become rampant in some societies. Living in fear with nebulous thoughts of "what if" or acting out of ignorance to get retribution creates a society of distrustful, power-hungry, controlling individuals who would rather shoot into oblivion than sit down and have an intelligent conversation. Disregard for human life and racial discord infiltrate our societies while fear and hatred expand and perpetuate violence. Hatred and violence create chaos and discord. Churches and other religious institutions and leaders such as Martin Luther King and Mahatma Gandhi have provided an alternative for violence offering peace and nonviolence. Many times fears are baseless. Our planet needs healing. When we focus on peace and harmony and respect each other's difference, we can celebrate in Unity Consciousness where we can live in peace and freedom. Some ills in our will society will continue until we find ways to heal ourselves on the inside. Humanity is sorely in need of peace and new ways of working together for the benefit of all sentient beings. Finding the positives in our world and people are important to create an atmosphere of love and joy.

Depression

Unfortunately, depression is rampant amongst the inmate population, who often experience extreme depression. Depressive disorder or clinical depression is a common mental condition involving a persistent low or sad mood and/or lack of pleasure or interest in normal activity. Depression is different from the typical sad or "down" moods that everyone experiences. It can be triggered by trauma or loss, or can be a matter of brain chemistry, with no identifiable exterior cause. If depression is severe and interferes with daily life, antidepressant medication and/or therapy can help. Other members of society also suffer from this illness, which can be debilitating especially in times of stress.

Inmates can also suffer from "situational depression," brought on by the stressful experiences of prison. Depression is one of the five stages of incarceration which include denial, anger, bargaining, and acceptance; similar to the stages of grief described by psychiatrist Elisabeth Kubler-Ross. Feelings of loneliness and sadness can come from separation from family and loved ones. Sometimes just a sense of malaise can throw an inmate into a negative spiral. I have come to know the inmates who attended my classes, and I can sometimes see and feel a sense of sadness in their eyes. My heart goes out to them because there is a sense that they are missing the key human element, love. Everyone wants to be loved. It is a natural human emotion. Some of the inmates have mental disorders other than clinical depression, which exacerbates the situation. Their psychological wellbeing can take a toll while they are incarcerated. The depression does not stop after they are released back into society. While some turn inward during meditation and prayer, others are unable to find coping mechanisms and are likely to turn to outside influences to numb the emotional pain.

Inmates cry just like anyone else. In men's prisons, some try to hide their tears and sorrow and have actually told me that they do not want to cry in prison because it might show weakness. Unfortunately, as children, boys are often told to be a man. They grow up thinking that it is not okay to cry. I think it is healthy to shed some tears, from time to time. The most balanced men are those who can laugh and cry. Either tears of sadness or tears of joy, emotions need to be expressed from time to time in an effort to let go of the stress associated with them. Therefore, I would encourage the inmates to express their sadness in a safe space. It is not conducive to our bodies and mind to suppress negative emotions.

Once people begin to understand their own natures and take responsibility for their actions, self awareness increases and a sense of wellbeing is experienced. Those who have learned meditation techniques often use their skills to defuse conflicts around them. The pranayama breathing practice based on the rhythm and count of 4:16:8 is one of the easiest, most effective, and fastest practices for calming tension. Expanded awareness sheds light on old negative patterns, habits, and obsessive thoughts. Negative emotions such as anger, frustration, and anxiety dissipate at a much faster rate when one becomes aware of thoughts, actions, and emotions.

Bringing light into the darkness of prisons has given me a sense of euphoria knowing that I am fulfilling part of my mission. We all are connected with Divinity. What we do with our free will, choices we make, and our circumstances all contribute to our success or failure.

Learning to differentiate between what is real and what is unreal is one of the keys to finding freedom in bondage. Holding onto fear, anger, and victimhood is not useful and keeps us stuck. Learning to live in the present moment is more difficult than it seems. Letting go of fear and finding peace amidst the chaos in life can provide us with a sense of freedom from the challenges and vicissitudes of life. Being sent to prison provides challenges that are unlike any other experiences in the outer world.

The word... "**Guilty!**" rings out in the courtroom when the jury determines you have committed a crime. It must be proven beyond a reasonable doubt. That word can provoke fear or resignation. It can also affect the body leading to hypertension and heart disease. But what happens if the defendant is innocent and has to pay for the crime committed by someone else? Throughout history there have been stories of people spending years or even life in prison for crimes they did not commit such as the verdict that sent five young Black and Hispanic 14, 15 and 16 year old teens to prison. They were convicted and sent to prison for assaulting and raping a white woman who was jogging in Central Park in New York on April 19, 1989. These boys became known as Central Park Five. They were later exonerated when DNA linked a man to the crime and he confessed his own guilt resulting in the boys' release. These five innocent young Black and Hispanic teenagers paid for that crime and spent five to 13 years in prison until they were exonerated.

When the real attacker confessed that he committed the crime, the teens had already spent years in prison. How did that affect them? These young innocent boys had their lives forever damaged by the guilty verdict. A guilty verdict deeply impacts the perpetrator's wellbeing. Their lives will never be the same. Some are sent into a negative spiral of disbelief, followed by anger and fear. Their

Doreena Durbin

families are also affected. They lost their son, brother, or nephew. What happens to the human psyche in situations like these?

Some Native Americans have said our souls make contracts with the Creator prior to taking birth to teach us lessons for our highest good. The idea of choosing our parents and life circumstances helps to teach us these life lessons. Everyone plays various roles in life. Mother, father, business man, entertainer, or spiritual leader— all teach us various aspects of ourselves. Being attached to our roles will only bring us stress when the job or role disappears.

102

CHAPTER 16

CLASSES

The following events took place before, during, or after each class:

I kept journals following each class, which partially became the contents of this book. At the time I did not intend to use them to write this book but once I realized the value it could have for the benefit of the inmates, I decided it would be worthwhile. I believed that the institution, the guards, and prison staff would also be beneficiaries while working in a less tense environment. This book could also serve as a reminder of what the inmates and I shared in the classes. The inmates have made enormous contributions during our classes and for that I am very grateful. I have asked those who contributed their stories for their permission to include them in this book. To respect their privacy, I purposely did not use their names. Topics of discussion rose spontaneously while I sensed the energy in the room. I intuitively chose topics based on the energy they were emanating based on their interests, needs, and challenges. Prison checks, quarantines, and lockdowns often conflicted with our classes but that did not stop the classes from taking place. I learned to flow and to take everything in stride. Prior to beginning each class, I always asked for guidance and protection from Source as I invoked prayer and positive energy.

Doreena Durbin

April 4, 2023 - You are worthy! You are Divine!

About a dozen inmates and a couple of guards gathered outside of the library to participate in my first class. As the inmates began to filter in, I welcomed them and instructed them to have a seat. I was informed that prisons in Texas do not have air conditioning! Texas can be quite brutal in the summer with temperatures rising to 100 degrees or more. It was already getting hot. I learned that the library was one of the few places in the prison that had an air conditioner. I was grateful because I have succumbed to heat stroke on several occasions whenever it gets too hot. I learned that the buildings in which the dormitories are situated are made of metal and there is only one large fan in the dorms. As we settled in, one of the inmates commented that this was the first time in four years that he sat in a comfortable chair. They use plastic folding chairs in the chapel. I thought... in the spiritual world and as Divine beings and heirs of God, we all deserve to be treated fairly and with compassion.

The energy was strong and palpable. I felt a sense of vibrancy. I made it clear that for everyone's safety following the Covid pandemic, that I would greet them with "Namaste." I explained that there would be no touching, hand shaking, or hugging. I put my hands together and demonstrated the "Namaste" prayer pose, which is commonly used in Asian cultures. I explained that the word "Namaste" literally means, *I honor the place in you in which the entire Universe dwells. When you are in that place in you and I am in that place in me, we are One.* My words flowed from somewhere deep inside of me.

I wanted the inmates to feel comfortable and excited about learning something new that they may never have the opportunity to experience again. As an empath and intuitive I sensed the room and attuned to their needs. I wanted to provide them with a way out of the drudgeries of living in the harsh prison environment where their freedom is taken away. I had no idea what I was going to say but I felt guided and confident that once I began speaking the words would flow effortlessly. The main thing I wanted to convey was that they are worthy and Divine. Letting go of guilt is part of the healing process. Most of the inmates were new to meditation and were drawn to my class by some unseen force to learn this valuable ancient practice. Perhaps they were intrigued by the flier that was posted around the prison. A guard stood watch from a hallway outside the library. This was my first class and I did not know what to expect. *I literally had a captive audience!*

I looked around the room and saw inmates of various races, ethnic groups, and age groups. Many of them were covered with tattoos on their faces, arms, and heads. I learned that tattooed tears under eyes can signify losing a loved one while being incarcerated. It can also represent gang affiliation or having been involved in an act of murder. Living in a prison doesn't give inmates many choices. Free will is literally taken away from them.

In my peripheral vision, I noticed two young inmates sitting in the back corner of the room trying to hide behind a pole. They were demonstratively affectionate towards each other as they sat side by side, giggling like young school girls. One of them put his hand on his friend's knee while the other one was caressing his friend's leg. They seemed happy to find a few moments of joy. As they continued talking and giggling, I sensed they were beginning to disrupt the class. The guards were starting to notice from the large window. I knew I had to take control and spoke up…"Guys, do one of you want to come up here and teach this class? Please respect the other guys who are here to learn." The other inmates were sitting in front of them and didn't turn around to see what was going on between them. I asked them to engage in the class with the rest of us. There were no more interruptions. They re-engaged and I continued talking.

I wanted to share that the separation from society does not mean that they are separated from God. Like drops in the ocean we are all part of the Divine plan of the Universe. I knew that if they practiced meditation on a regular basis their awareness would increase. By turning their attention from the chaotic outer world to their peaceful inner worlds their spirits would be uplifted and they could experience some peace and happiness, even while serving time in prison. Our spirits are forever free and no one can ever control them or take them away from us. No one! Separation is in the mind. God is omnipresent and resides in every cell of our bodies and within all animate life forms. Our frequencies and vibrations become lighter and more refined when we meditate regularly.

I spoke about how we are placed in various life circumstances. Instead of fighting we can look for what is propelling us forward. Is it the ego? We must make the best of our situations and circumstances. For every adversity there is an opportunity. We must get away from judgments of ourselves and others. Many have imprisoned themselves by reliving their misdeeds. Fear is rampant in many communities causing mistrust and hatred of the other. We must try to find the good in people and become integrated within ourselves by connecting with our own Divinity, so we can perceive the Divinity in others. Focusing on the mud will keep us stuck in our own muddy hell holes. The stars are always there; we just need to realize that we all come from the same source. We are all seeking joy, peace, and freedom. Most people live in the past or the future instead of enjoying the present moment, which is where true peace and happiness can be found.

The mind is filled with so many memories of the past: the good, the bad, and the ugly. We expend so much energy thinking about the past and if we could go back and change it—would we do anything differently? Spending so much time stuck in thought wormholes of blame and shame will not bring us joy. It will only perpetuate the very things we are trying to avoid. So accept the fact that we have some misdeeds and there is nothing we can do to change it. Are we going to waste our precious time and energy knowing that we cannot change the past? That will only create insanity. We must look to ourselves for forgiveness and start from today on to begin a new life with determination and purpose. Think about how many people in the world who are in much worse circumstances. Be grateful that you have a life and more opportunities to learn and grow. Instead of focusing on your suffering, begin with one small step each day and focus on service. Think about what you can do to alleviate the suffering of others. Offer your prison brothers good energy and bring them to their own inner lights where freedom from bondage can be found. The stars exist in the sky and the cosmos. We just have to move the clouds of darkness away and look up to see them. In other words we need to get out of our own way. Those who have eyes to see, use them! Those who have ears to hear, listen! Those who have a voice, use it for the greater good of humanity by speaking truth.

I am aware that many meditation instructors ask their students to get into the traditional cross legged Indian pose as is often seen in pictures of meditators. Some have their index finger and thumb together. However, this pose becomes difficult for people who have knee injuries or arthritis, and the elderly who suffer stiffness in their bones. It would also be difficult for people in prisons due to lack of private space, and a chaotic noisy environment. I wanted to make it as easy and comfortable as possible so they would not be limited in finding a time and place to meditate. Also, drawing attention to themselves might cause them to be bothered, ridiculed, or teased by other inmates. I suggested that they simply sit on a chair with their feet on the floor and hands together. They could also lie on their bunk beds. Their hands and arms should be by their sides to get maximum relaxation benefits. Meditating in dorms may be challenging because they share their dormitories with 56 other inmates, so finding solitude is very difficult. I asked them to sit comfortably and I would guide them through a relaxation exercise in paying attention to where they are holding onto their stress. I guided them into a body scan. Starting at the top of the head we worked down to the neck, shoulders, arms, torso, legs, and feet. While they were relaxing each body part, I instructed them to pay attention to where they are holding onto their stress. By the end of the exercise one of the inmates said that he did not realize how tight his shoulders were until he put his attention on them.

Following the body scan, we settled into silence and I guided them into a meditation using the breath as a focal point. I instructed them that each and every time their attention drifted onto thoughts they should return their attention back to their breathing. They would feel their breath slowing down significantly. Some would become aware that their breathing becomes more shallow and slows down almost to a standstill. I assured them that their autonomic nervous systems would not allow them to stop breathing completely. This meditation practice is simple and easy to do and has a nice calming effect.

As I spoke, I noticed that some of the inmates were wide eyed when I began telling them that they are worthy and Divine just as everyone else in the human race. I wondered how many times they were told that in their lives. Parents, law enforcement, or others in their lives may have beaten them down, but they are still worthy of love and respect because of their connection with the Creator. The inmates appeared very engaged and attentive. Afterwards several guys shared that they enjoyed my class and that it was very different from any other class they had ever attended, especially at the prison. They said that no one else in the prison had ever talked with them about the things that I shared. A feeling of satisfaction filled my being when I saw their eyes light up with childlike wonder. I was reminded about the first time I heard my teacher speak decades ago. I was mesmerized and fascinated by his wisdom and knowledge. I'm sure my eyes lit up too!

April 18, 2023

I arrived about 30 minutes early. I was not allowed to bring my cell phone, books, or anything else. I trusted that the Universe had a plan for me. I signed in and was body searched by a female officer. After being instructed to leave my driver's license with someone at the second security gate, I walked alone down the long courtyard past inmates gathered in small groups or lined up on the sidewalk, going to wherever the guards were accompanying them. As I got to the end, I thought I might have missed the sidewalk that goes to the chapel so I asked one of the inmates if he could point the way. I followed his pointed finger and continued walking until I reached near the end. When I opened a door I was shocked to see inmates in various parts of the building. Some were sitting, others were lying on bunk beds, some were watching TV, and others were sitting at small tables playing card games or conversing. I had mistakenly opened the wrong door! I quickly realized it was a dormitory! I'm sure the guys were just as surprised as me seeing a woman standing at the doorway of their dorm. I was embarrassed so I quickly closed the door. Once I recovered and realized that I was in the wrong building, I thought ...there are no accidents. I got a glimpse into the challenges they face when trying to find space and time to meditate. I went back outside and continued walking down the courtyard to the next gate. I wondered if I would be able to energetically protect myself from the negative energies in the harsh prison environment. I wondered if I would feel drained of energy on my drive home. While walking to the end of the half mile courtyard I heard metal gates slamming behind me. A guard yelled and I witnessed an inmate being thrown to the ground and handcuffed. I knew meditation could replace fear with love and despair with hope. A feeling of hope was in the air.

I was happy to see the Chaplain who was waiting for me so he could unlock the last security gate. After entering the library, I asked him if I could get a microphone so I could be heard in the back of the room. He sent an inmate into the library to set it up. I could tell he had some experience and chatted with him while waiting for the other inmates to show up. He was very polite and respectful. I asked him if he worked in electronics on the outside before he came to prison. He told me that he never had formal training in electronics but was grateful that his stepfather taught him. I wondered if his skills had given him value while serving time at the prison. Within minutes other inmates started coming in and sat on the cushioned chairs around the library. The room was a perfect size and comfortably fit the 20-25 inmates who would be attending my class. The first two inmates who showed up were a short statured Irish guy and a tall Hispanic man who was covered with tattoos. He sat against the wall on my right. I asked if any of them had an opportunity to meditate since our first class. Most of them didn't. D said he saw Reverend R and told him about our class. The Reverend asked if the instructor was named "Doreena" with two "ee"s. When the Reverend acknowledged that I was the same woman he had invited to the prison several years ago (prior to the Covid shutdown), he was pleased and gave him a high five and replied, "She finally made it!" Reverend R asked how he liked the class and D responded, "Yes, I like it. She's the real deal!" I later learned that the inmate was a practicing meditator with years of experience. He had spent some time in an Ashram prior to incarceration. Reverend R. asked him if he knew what day of the week I would be teaching because he wanted to stop by and say, "Hello."

I welcomed the new inmates and the previous group who came to my first class. I started the class by asking what their greatest challenges are when trying to meditate in the prison environment. They said their greatest challenge was dealing with the constant distractions and it was difficult to find quiet time and conducive spaces. They said that the lights throughout the prison are on 24/7. Some tie a sock around their heads to block out light while they're sleeping, but then guards come in throughout the night and sometimes push them to see if they are alive and breathing.

I spoke about *samskaras,* the Sanskrit word which means impressions on the mind. I spoke about the three layers of the mind: the conscious mind, subconscious mind, and the superconscious mind. We began with a brief body scan as we started from the head and ended at the toes. I asked them to pay attention to where they were holding onto their stress as I went through each body part. This is similar to the Yoga Nidra exercise where you are lying on the floor in the Asana yoga position. Instead, the inmates were sitting in chairs. I taught them how to do the rhythmic breathing practice. My spiritual teacher explained that if they could stand outside the Universe they would feel the Universe pulsating at the rate of 4:16:8. Doing this powerful breathing practice several times a day would give them a sense of peace and calm by aligning themselves with Universal energy. After several rounds I gently guided them into a meditation focusing on the breath.

I wanted the class to be interactive. I asked for a show of hands for anyone who had previously experienced meditation. Several guys raised their hands. I allayed the fears of Christians who thought that meditation would conflict with their Christian faith. I explained that meditation can actually enhance whatever religion they followed because it would increase their understanding, thereby deepening their faiths. One of the inmates, D, appeared to know a lot about meditation and often nodded in agreement as I explained a little about the history and the benefits. He said that he had attended an Ashram that taught a form of Samadhi meditation. He seemed to be an adept and supported and confirmed what I was saying. We meditated on the breath (10-15 minutes). One guy said he became aware of a bird chirping when he was meditating. Another said he felt a sense of peace and calm. I told them they could lie on the carpeted floor if they wished. It was an amazing meditation session! We ended on a positive note and I walked out of the building and down the long courtyard feeling euphoric. I found my niche. I felt that I destined to be offering meditation practices to prisoners.

For the next 2 weeks the prison was on lockdown due to an incident that broke out among inmates. I was informed that I would receive an email when the lockdown was lifted. I could not resume my class until it was all clear.

May 23, 2023

My class was amazing! Twenty inmates showed up, including several new guys. A tall Muslim guy with a white Kufi hat, popped his head in the door and asked if my class was exclusive for Christians and if it was based on Christian theology. He identified as a Muslim and didn't want it to interfere with his faith.

I explained some of the benefits of meditation. I read a few quotes from Nelson Mandela and my teacher, Gururaj Ananda Yogi. We did the breathing exercise, followed by a meditation. I gave them a simple mantra, which had a calming effect due to the vibrations in each syllable. I spoke about the three layers of the mind, impressions, (samskaras), and energy. I spoke about childhood trauma and noticed some of them shaking their heads affirming that they had some negative experiences. I told them how important they are and that they are valuable as human beings. As Eckhart Tolle said: *"You are here to enable the Divine purpose of the of the Universe to unfold. That is how important you are!"* I told them that life is a school and how to look for the good in so called negative life experiences—that even the prison sentence they were given is teachable and can be a learning experience when viewed from a different perspective. Learning to meditate while serving time is a good experience. Perhaps they may never have the opportunity to be exposed to meditation on the outside. One of the guys shared his positive meditation experience and that he thought the meditation lasted for about 5 minutes when it actually lasted 15-20 minutes.

I shared an experience of a car crash that I had when a truck hit me head-on on an expressway during a Chicago winter storm. I spoke about the power of Grace and gave them some tips and ideas about how to stay in the present moment to endure their prison experience, or when they were feeling off balance. I told them to use any of the three techniques that I taught (meditation on breath, mantra, or pranayama). Getting in touch with their inner selves is a powerful way to experience a calm body and mind. They seemed grateful for the spiritual light coming into the prison. I understood that although it is difficult to find the time and space to meditate, freedom and inner silence can still be found. They had the freedom to choose whichever practice would be most conducive for them.

When the class ended, everyone stood up to clap. I didn't expect that. I felt a little shy because I felt the words I spoke were being channeled through me. I was just an instrument. Some did the Namaste pose I taught them. They thanked me for coming.

June 6, 2023

The Reverend stopped by to talk about his program in the faith based dormitory. He again asked if I could teach his group every other week. I told him it was difficult since I drove 150 miles round trip to the prison but I would do my best and would let him know. I realized the value and benefits of my program so I wanted to do as much as possible.

We had a small powerful group today. I was informed that the guards wouldn't let some of the inmates out of their dorms because there was a prison check. The guys who were there asked great questions. We conversed about awareness, vibrations in animate and inanimate objects, as well as the vibrations of our names. Some were curious about the Sanskrit language so we discussed its origins as well as other languages and the history of various religions. Two of the books that I was reintroduced to by one of the inmates was, *The Four Agreements* by Don Miguel Ruiz and *Angel Words* by Doreen Virtue. I asked one of the practitioners of Islam if chants are invoked in the Muslim religion. He said that

113

some chants are in the Qur'an, their sacred Islamic texts, which help connect them with the Divine.

We meditated on a mantra that when invoked, creates positive vibrations. Four of the guys lay on the floor but about halfway through the meditation they sat up. It must have been uncomfortable since they were not allowed to bring pillows or cushions, which could be used for malicious intentions. Our conversations and discussions were interactive.

I stood up and told them that I wanted to get on the road because it was going to rain. I didn't want to endure a three hour commute driving in the rain and in the dark. As we were preparing to leave we gathered in the hallway and waited for the guard to unlock the gate while chatting. We walked together down the courtyard. I felt like I was supported by my "posse." I heard voices trailing behind, "Drive carefully!" Be safe!" The inmates stopped about half way down the courtyard and continued to their dorms or wherever else they were going. I was allowed to continue walking until I reached the end. I picked up my driver's license at the last security gate and walked to the parking lot to find my car.

I got caught in a heavy torrential rain storm. It was pounding my windshield! I couldn't see a foot in front of me on that dark rainy night. I could not pull over to the side of the road so I just endured and carried on with intense focus. I just wanted to get home. My windshield wipers were unable to keep up with the pouring rain to provide me with a clear view. Trust and faith was all I had. The wind picked up and I felt my car swaying, which made the car even more difficult to control. I began to pray and silently asked God for protection. Then I thought of one of my favorite songs, "You!ll Never Walk Alone" and began to sing out loud…"*When you walk through a storm, hold your head up high and don't be afraid of the dark. At the end of the storm there's a golden sky and the sweet silver song of a lark. Walk on through the wind, walk on through the rain, though your dreams be tossed and blown. Walk on, walk on, with hope in your heart and you'll never walk alone, you'll never walk alone."* I had trust and faith that I would arrive home.

I heard the inmates telling me to "stay safe". I felt their supportive presence, which helped carry me to safety. I arrived home safe and sound after a 2.5 hour commute.

Inmates have reputations for being violent and angry but I have not been exposed to anyone at the prison who exhibited those tendencies, with the exception of one of the inmates who stared at me with eyes that reminded me of someone who seemed to have nefarious intentions. In retrospect, I realized he reminded me of a gang member that I encountered in a dicey Chicago neighborhood.

June 20, 2023

It was 100 degrees as I walked through the courtyard. There were lots of delays at several gates due to a shift change for the guards and employees. I had to wait in the sun for the guards to unlock the gates before I could continue to the library where Reverend R was waiting for me. He wanted to know when I could participate in his faith based Christian ministries program where approximately 200 inmates come for his sermons.

I had a small class today. I was told that the guards were not releasing the inmates who signed up for my class from their dorms. The inmates who were present were very attentive. I brought *The Four Agreements* book and one of the guys asked if I could read some of it to them. I read several pages, then we meditated on the breath for 20 minutes.

July 4, 2023

No class today. I was supposed to travel to the AMS retreat in Missouri but a tornado hit the facilities and blew the roof off.

Too much energy blew the roof off? I found that to be a little humorous, especially since we were all meditators and emanated a tremendous amount of energy. Thank God none of us had arrived yet! We were all safe in our homes.

July 11, 2023

Today was the best class yet! Eight new inmates showed up as well as the "regulars" so our class size was full. Everyone was about 30 minutes late due to a "prison check." I greeted the new guys and asked if any of them had experienced meditation before attending my class. None of them had. I asked their names and asked them to sign in.

I talked about meditation, the brain, the layers of the mind, samskaras, and presence. I read a paragraph on "Freedom" from *The Four Agreements.* We talked about Oneness and the family, and societal agreements we assumed from our parents, teachers, and people within our communities. I told them that even though they're in the prison system that nothing or nobody can ever control or take away their spirits because they are always free.

We started with a body scan, then shifted into a 20 minute meditation on the breath. We ended with the breathing practice. I tried a Zen type of meditation with my eyes half open for the new participants. I needed to be aware of my surroundings. One young inmate asked how he can get rid of obsessive ruminating thoughts. I told him that meditation practices were very helpful since they infuse the body and mind with spiritual energy. One of the analogies I used was to envision a glass of dirty water sitting under a dripping faucet. The dirty water becomes clearer and clearer with each drop of clean water that falls into the glass. Like that analogy, the mind can be cleansed and purified with oxygenated breathing and with mantra meditation.

I had the opportunity to speak with D about my vision, which I put in my proposal, that I would identify an inmate who was a meditation adept who might be able to continue my classes once I'm gone. He liked the idea and said that he might be able to do it under the Prison Life Coaching program. He will look into it.

A young man named B sought me out after our class and was waiting by the security gate as I was preparing to walk into the courtyard. He said he was a practitioner of Buddhist Metta (loving kindness) meditation. He wanted to thank me for coming to teach the inmates. He seemed very appreciative.

July 25, 2023

It was 109 degrees outside! Several new guys showed up. One of the younger inmates with a nice personality and a big smile and childlike energy asked if he could lie on the floor during meditation. I said yes. He couldn't seem to find a spot and was crawling around the floor under the table and chairs. Then one of the guards looked inside the window outside of the library spotted him. He pointed at him and gestured to me to see if he had my approval to be on the floor. I gave him a thumbs up and gestured, he's ok. One of the young African American inmates raised his hand after the meditation and said he was having a difficult time with obsessive thoughts and wasn't able to get into the meditation. We talked about thoughts for a while and how they come and go during the meditative state.

The Chaplain was waiting for me when I walked out of the library with the guys to head out to the courtyard. He gave me a certificate of appreciation signed by him and the Warden. I thanked him then walked with the inmates to the first gate. The young man who was having difficulty with negative thoughts was waiting by the gate to talk with me. I noticed that he seemed withdrawn for the past couple of weeks. He shared that he lost his mother two weeks ago. My heart went out to him because he wasn't able to see her before she passed. I comforted him by saying that love never dies and her spirit was still with him. We talked for several minutes then we had to part ways because he wasn't allowed past the next security gate.

August 1, 2023

When I arrived it was 111 degrees! I learned that the Texas Governor did not approve air conditioners in prisons! I expressed my anger. I thought that was inhumane and wondered if any inmates lost their lives due to heat stroke. I also learned that their dorm buildings were made of metal! Fortunately the library was air conditioned. I was grateful and I am certain the inmates were grateful too.

D asked if I was familiar with a couple of groups who had meditation programs. He was hoping to be paroled in the near future and asked if I would be willing to speak with a couple of people at a Unity Church to see if they could continue my program after I moved out of state.

August 15, 2023

It was another great day at the prison. I arrived 30 minutes late in scorching 100 degree weather. I was rushing to go inside! I waited longer than usual to go through the searching process because the changing of the guards was in progress. After getting body searched, removing my shoes, and having my clear plastic file opened and looked through, I walked quickly down the courtyard to the end and saw the Chaplain waiting for me with a smiling face. I told him that I dropped my green volunteer badge somewhere along the walk. He said the inmates were waiting for me.

I went into the library and I was full of energy and excitement as I was greeted by 10-12 inmates with smiling faces. I said, "Hello guys! Sorry, I'm late!" I was caught up in traffic due to three auto accidents. I told them that I had to practice what I teach and used the breathing practice to calm down while driving in the horrible traffic through Dallas.

118

I asked how they were all doing and then I jumped right in without delay. I informed them that I found someone that would continue the meditation when I'm gone. D was happy to hear that I had pursued this person because he felt it would be conducive to continuing the meditation classes. At my previous class, he had written down the names of two people who taught Samadhi meditation. He couldn't give me their contact information since he didn't have the internet, so I offered to contact the meditation center to inquire about someone who could teach meditation.

I explained a few things about meditation as a review for the "regulars" and reminded the newer guys—such as not meditating too soon after a meal, treating sounds like thoughts, etc. I asked if anyone had any meditations on their own since our last class. One of the inmates, B, said he has been meditating twice a day and felt that he was benefitting. I noticed that his eyes were brighter and his face was softer. I asked others what they were getting from the class. Nearly everyone spoke. I noticed an older man with a beard who has never spoken at any of my classes. He always appeared sad. I made a point of asking him if he would like to share. He always participated by meditating with the group but had nothing to say. I energetically surrounded him with healing energy.

We meditated for about 15 minutes; then I read a page from one of Gururaj's transcripts. I asked if they would like to see a picture of Gururaj. I passed a Namaste picture around the room. I brought Elkhart Tolle's book *Silence Speaks*. The young Hispanic inmate (J) with a big infectious smile and sweet childlike energy sat in the chair directly in front of me. He said that yesterday was his 33rd birthday. I wished him a happy birthday. I noticed his eyes weren't closed when we were meditating so I handed him Tolle's book to read while the other guys meditated. Afterwards, he asked if I could read something from the chapter "Nature" in Tolle's book. Gururaj's small Namaste photo fell out. One of the guys noticed his name on the large photo and said his name out loud. I stayed for 30 minutes longer to make up for the delayed start time.

I finished by asking them if they could share some of the things that stood out for them in the teachings. D, J, C, B, and others shared. We ended with my telling them that I think of them often, see their faces throughout the week, and send them healing energy. My heart expands every time I think of them.

We stood together and waited in the hallway for about 15 minutes until a guard came to unlock the security gate J (the sweet inmate with the infectious smile) asked me about my makeup. He liked that my eyeliner looked nice and thin and said that I must have a steady hand since it was nicely applied. I purposely don't wear a lot of makeup when I go to the prison but wearing it since childhood during my musical stage life, I don't feel complete without it. We were standing in close proximity to each other and in front of the other guys he asked if I use Estee Lauder makeup. I said "No...do you?" It was obvious that he didn't have an ounce of embarrassment asking me that question in front of the other guys. I love his sweet exuberant energy! He talked about how he loved putting on makeup. Then we walked together down the first part of the courtyard. As I continued walking I heard several of the inmates say, "Drive carefully" and "Be safe." Other inmates were walking in lines in the courtyard and nodded or spoke to me, and some of them also told me to "Be safe!"

I felt like the classes were making a difference and there seemed to be a ripple effect. I was happy to see a gray tabby cat walking through the courtyard. Animals seem to sense when people are needing them on an emotional level.

August 29, 2023

Incredible experience today! Arrived at 2:00 pm (an hour early) to meet my potential replacement (S) in the parking lot at the entrance of the prison. We got patted down and body searched, removed shoes and belongings. We left our driver's licenses at the window. We walked to the middle outside counter where five or six guards were standing around talking. I asked if someone could call the Chaplain, to open the last gate. One of them said that a different program was using the library until our class started and that we should wait in the dining hall where guards were clustered around tables talking. There was a television and a big fan for the guards to cool off in the 100 degree Texas weather. S and I sat down and talked about the program.

We walked outside back to the desk/counter where six or seven guards were gathered.

I asked again for them to check and see if someone could let us in. Then I saw the Reverend who was very happy to see me. He gave me a big hug and I told him that I was looking for him to introduce S, my replacement. He welcomed her. Then we told him that we were nearly 45 minutes late for my class. He shouted to one of the guards to get someone to open the gate so we could get into the library.

We sat waiting for another 20-30 minutes then finally the inmates started walking in.

About 16 guys showed up. I was happy to see them and it seemed mutual. I introduced S to D who started talking with her. We waited for other inmates to show up, then after about ten minutes, I told them we were going to get started. I began speaking about their value as human beings and how important it was to have self respect. I knew I was being led by grace as the right words seemed to flow effortlessly. Some of the guys were excited when I told them that I brought their certificates of completion for finishing my class. I got a kick out of sweet J who was flaunting his feminine side. We had a nice session and I tried to demonstrate for S how I conducted the class. The guys were very receptive. I expressed that we may have different teachers and that they will be learning different things from S, and she will be teaching in her own style. I shared that I honor all of my teachers and felt that everyone has something to teach. Then I explained that when I read their names they should come up to receive their certificates one inmate at a time. It turned into a very special award ceremony. They were thrilled and were smiling and having fun as they clapped for each other upon receiving their certificates. I made them so they could show them to the parole board as an accomplishment. I made a point of looking at each and every one of them directly in their eyes and sharing something positive I saw in them, such as J's big beautiful smile and joyful spirit. I thanked D for all of his help in supporting me by corroborating much of my teaching. What an awesome experience watching the happiness and joy on their faces! Some of the guys shook my hand or fist bumped and thanked me. It was a very rewarding experience! Then I asked if anyone wanted to share something that they learned and would carry with them into their futures. D talked about how he was supposed to be paroled but was told he had to serve another year. He was actually pleased and said that he would not have had the opportunity to take my class if he had been released earlier so he was grateful. Another guy said he learned a lot and had since found a group of guys at the prison he resonated with. Some said that when they see someone that they met in our class, they greet each other and are happy that they have a camaraderie with each other. One guy said that he feels the Oneness that we are all linked together. I shared that we are all like one big family. All different beautiful races, religions and ethnic backgrounds. I asked J what he will take with him and without skipping a beat, he shouted, "Rajananda!"

After taking a few breaths we meditated for about 15 minutes. I reminded them about some points of meditation and the importance of regularity so they should try to do it everyday in prison. We ended the class. The thin white guard told us to wait in the hallway while he called a guard at the other end to unlock the gate. We stood outside for about 10 minutes waiting and chatting. J commented on my makeup again and said I should wear more blush. He noticed my very minimal amount of eye shadow and liner. I saw he had dark mottled looking eyeshadow and asked him about it. He said he has to improvise in prison and used "shoe polish."

I led the way as we walked toward the gate down the courtyard. I heard several inmates from my team say, "'Drive carefully" or "Be safe." S and I continued to walk further down the courtyard. There were about 200 inmates walking between the yellow lines on both sides of the courtyard looking at us. Most spoke after hearing the other inmates from my class telling us to drive safely. I responded with "Bless you" to a number of inmates we passed along the way.

September 5, 2023

The Chaplain sent me an email during the week and asked if I could do another class so he could say goodbye. He said the inmates also wanted to say goodbye. I saw him in the lobby when I got checked in. There were a lot of guards in the lobby due to a shift change.

The inmates and I met at the last gate and waited for a guard to let us in. We had a lively chat. They were pleased that I came two weeks in a row. I told them I wanted to come to say goodbye. I saw CV, who said he didn't get his certificate even though he had attended my classes. (I seemed to recall that he came late for a couple of classes and more than likely, he forgot to sign in). A few of the inmates concurred that he was present so I told him I would make him a certificate and mail it to A's attention so he could give it to him.

D asked where I got the slogan, "Get An Inner Life." He liked it and thought it was very appropriate for the class. I told him that one of the meditators from my meditation group came up with that very appropriate slogan, which I thought was perfect to use for incarcerated individuals on the spiritual path. I took out a copy of the flier and went through the text during the class to see if we covered everything. We did! Then I talked to them about all of the practices that they had experienced.

Doreena Durbin

We started with three rounds of pranayama; then I introduced the chant. They asked me to write it on the white board. We chanted for about 5-10 minutes. They liked it! I spoke with them about the candle meditation and drew a large dot on the whiteboard. It was difficult to see for the guys sitting in the back row. Besides, there was too much light in the room! The guards do not want complete darkness in the prison and would more than likely come in to turn on at least one or two ceiling lights. We shifted our focus and meditated for 15 minutes on the breath.

Great session covering everything that I taught in previous classes!

October 24, 2023

S couldn't make it so I told her that I would teach the class today. Nothing was planned so as usual my words flowed effortlessly as I began to speak. I didn't bring any notes or props, just my driver's license, which was left at the third gate, my car fob, and a comb. It was dark and raining heavily on the 2-3 hour commute.

I arrived 15 minutes late, checked in, and walked briskly down the courtyard to the library, then was told they were waiting in the chapel. I walked down the hall and entered the chapel where a large group of inmates were sitting on the chairs and chatting. I asked them all to follow me into the library. It was smaller and I liked the intimate setting for our meditation classes. The Chaplain greeted me warmly and the guys seemed somewhat surprised to see me. They were expecting my replacement.

We settled in and began talking. I was glad to see familiar faces, D, Z, B, J, C, C, etc., as well as a few new inmates. Z and several other guys said they missed me. I asked them what they would like the topic of our class to be. I told them that we could talk about philosophy, spirituality, religion, or any other topics they might be interested in. I gave them a rundown of the various meditation practices with tips about not eating a heavy meal

124

prior to meditating. We spoke about thoughts, etc. One asked about pranayama. Another wanted to know about the Native American experience I had when I attended an intertribal pow wow in Wisconsin with two Buddhist monks. The last surviving son of an Indian Chief asked if the monks and I would come with him about 25 miles away to their sacred burial ground to meditate on the property. He hoped to bring positive energy to avert the federal government from coming to mine there. I spoke about how Native Americans pray, treat all animals with respect, and use every part of the animal if they kill them for food, while offering prayers and gratitude.

I asked if any of them had questions about some of our previous classes. One of the guys asked about similarities of religions. I spoke about the AMS logo with religions circled around a candle flame. Z shared Muslim beliefs. He said they acknowledge Jesus as a great prophet. We named the nine major religions and I explained the essence of all religions being the same and how many of the wars in our world have been caused by the lack of understanding about religions. One inmate who had lots of tattoos fervently defended Christianity. I got the impression that he was a zealot wanting to be heard so I stopped to give him some space and an opportunity to quote scriptures.

D shared that he felt that since I started the meditation program the prison energy had changed for the better. They said there was more camaraderie and good energy and he felt a ripple effect reverberating through the prison environment. We started with three rounds of pranayama (the breathing practice) and a 15-20 minute meditation on the breath. We ended with the mantra and/or attention on the breath. I explained how to do tratak (visualization practice) and said we cannot do it in prison because lit candles are prohibited. However, they could use a different focal point like a large black dot on a whiteboard. They listened intently. When I told them the benefits, which included increased intuition and secreting melatonin, which is beneficial for sleep and developing the ability to focus, I sensed that they were eager to learn this visualization practice. One of the inmates asked if I could bring *The Four Agreements* to the next class and read a few chapters. I agreed. C, the young man still grieving the loss of his mother, fist bumped me, and a few guys shook my hand, which I finally allowed as I sensed more refined energy. Also, Covid was no longer an issue. Their faces appeared softer with more light shining in their eyes. That was a good sign that they were benefitting from the meditations. As we were walking into the hallway to go outside, the Chaplain stopped me and asked if I could teach my class on Nov. 7 as well any other classes I could fit into my schedule before I move. I agreed.

November 7, 2023

I arrived nearly 30 minutes late! I was so upset with myself for not leaving my house earlier. Then I ran into two traffic jams on the expressway due to multiple accidents. Upon arriving I rushed through the process of getting checked in. I was focused on getting to the library as quickly as possible where the inmates were waiting. A white woman shouted harshly to me stating ..."Who are you?" I acknowledged her but continued walking fast past her. I thought that it was unusual to see a female, especially since there were so few females at the prison. I didn't know who she was but I did not want to be delayed any longer. She did not have a uniform like he guards. She was wearing a black shirt and black pants. Then she said, "Stop! I am the Assistant Warden!" I felt like one of the inmates who was being detained for stepping out of line. She asked my name, where I was going, and what I was doing. I stopped and apologized, then gave her my name and the purpose for my visit. She allowed me to continue. I learned that she *was* the Assistant Warden. A new Warden would be coming within days.

The guys were happy to see me. I apologized for being late; then I settled in. I talked about our previous class. We discussed the essence of various religions and how the teachings were similar.

I brought a few copies of the Golden Rule according to multiple religions that I printed out, and asked a few of the inmates to read the descriptions. I asked Z to read about Islam. Two guys read the small print that described several other religions.

We talked about perceptions; then I provided examples on how everyone has different perceptions. One of the guys said, "That's how I got into prison because of my misconceptions." I read a few paragraphs from *The Four Agreements*. Then I used examples of perception including the story about the guy who went off to war and left his wife and infant son for several years until he returned from the war zone. The couple used to play shadow games on the wall in their bedroom making all sorts of shadow animals of rabbits, ducks, and birds while sharing stories. When the husband went to war his wife missed him so much that she continued playing shadow games, which brought her some comfort and company while waiting for her husband's return. The toddler used to hear his mother talking late at night. When her husband returned from war his wife was elated. To welcome him home she decided to cook a special meal. She wanted her husband and son to bond so she left them together at the house while she went shopping. The happy child was telling his father how he and his mother passed their time at home. The toddler told his father that his mom talked with somebody in her bed at the night. He falsely perceived that she shared her bed with another man. When his wife came home her husband was emotionally ice cold. His happiness turned to anger and he distanced himself from his wife. He refused to even look at her. She was so distraught when it carried on for days. She could not understand his emotional distance. She became desolate and severely depressed. Several weeks later she went to the bridge and jumped into the river, killing herself. Needless to say, her husband's misconception was the cause her suicide.

I spoke about the blackbirds flying above the courtyard during my last visit and how my perception was very different from some of the inmates. I saw the blackbirds as a good omen while some of the inmates began laughing and said they were reminded of the Alfred Hitchcock movie, "The Birds."

"Behold the birds in the air: they neither sow nor reap nor store away into barns, and yet your heavenly father feeds them. Are you not much more valuable than they? Can any one of you by worrying add a single hour to your life?" (Matt. 6:26-27).

The class was lively and uplifted. I saw the light in their eyes and joy on their faces and their eyes twinkled with delight. They uplifted me too.

I explained the visualization practice, which is beneficial for focusing the mind like a laser beam and how it is conducive for opening the third eye, which unfolds intuitive faculties. I told them that the visualization practice would be difficult to do in prison because candles are required in a dark room to get the maximum benefits and an after image when the eyes are opened. Since the lights have to be on 24/7 I told them I could teach them how to do the visualization practice, but they would need to wait until they got released to use a real candle. I asked B when he finds the best time to meditate. He told me that he meditates early in the morning on a daily basis. Before the chant, one of the guys asked if I could write the chant on the white board and say it a few times before we began. We chanted then we meditated for 10-15 minutes with our attention on the breath. Afterwards, I asked how many of them noticed the ease of shifting directly from the chant to the meditation and if they felt a deepening and more relaxation. They agreed that their meditations were deeper.

The Chaplain knocked on the window and gestured that it was time to wrap it up. I asked him if I could leave *The Four Agreements* with the inmates in the library. Z asked for it first and said he would make sure they all took turns reading it. The Chaplain shook my hand and several of the inmates shook my hand, held it, or fist bumped as we were preparing to leave. D did the Namaste pose. I realized that I had become more lax and less strict since I have softened my stance about the inmates touching me. It felt appropriate and good to be genuine so I didn't resist. The Chaplain asked if I could come back before the end of November to teach another class. I agreed.

As I was walking down the courtyard with D and another inmate, D said he thinks the reason that I'm still living in Texas is because the inmates need me and are benefiting from my program. I thought so too.

November 10, 2023

I fell down and broke my left clavicle. I sent the Chaplain an email informing him that I needed to cancel my Nov. 28 class. The very next day, I received Divine inspiration to start writing this book. I couldn't do anything else so I decided to follow the "command." I was excited and couldn't fall asleep as ideas began to enter my mind fast and furious as the creative process began flowing forth. I had a difficult time writing or typing with one hand because of the shoulder pain so I just took a few notes to remind me of the ideas popping into my head, which often occurred in the middle of the night. The next morning, I decided it was easier to use my laptop so I started typing using my right index finger one letter at a time. That is the method I used for weeks.

November 15, 2023

Following my accident, the decision to write a book about teaching meditation in a prison was coming to fruition.

On December 7, I received a call from the Chaplain asking me if I could come on December 19 because the inmates were missing me and our classes.

Doreena Durbin

December 19, 2023

When I entered the gates and started walking down the courtyard, several inmates asked me how I am doing after my recent clavicle fracture. I guess the word had gotten around about why I had to cancel my Nov. 28 class. I went into the library to settle in. One of the inmates, G, who helped me with setting up the microphone prior to one of my first classes, came in. I told him that I would not need the mic because I would speak louder. We chatted for about 20 minutes while waiting for the other inmates to arrive. He shared some of his life story with me about being adopted at age six and meeting his father for the last time. I asked him what tattoos of teardrops under inmates eyes represented and he said it signified gang affiliation. However, it could also mean losing loved ones while being incarcerated.

I was happy to see the inmates. Most had previously attended my class except for a new guy who came as a result of the nice young man whose mother passed away in July. He encouraged the new inmate to come. I welcomed him. I told the guys that I brought a book that I would like to donate as a gift for Christmas called *The Mastery of Self: A Toltec Guide to Personal Freedom* by Don Miguel Ruiz, Jr. I told them that I was writing a book and would be using some stories about our classes but I would not use their names to protect their privacy.

I spoke a little about meditation and turning the attention from the outer world to the inner world and asked if they found any opportunities to meditate. One inmate said it was difficult because of all of the distractions. I spoke about their value as human beings and how we are all sparks of the Divine and as such that we all have value since we are manifestations of God. "Did I not say, you are all Gods and Children of the most High?" (Psalm 64:18). We were born to serve humanity, in whichever way we can... even in prison. I spoke about looking for the silver lining in all adversities and how they need to focus on the positive rather than the negative. I told them my thoughts about why so many birds showed up for them above the prison. I shared that I thought of birds as messengers of God. I wondered if they came for each and every one of the 2,300 inmates to provide hope and healing— God hasn't given up on them or forgotten them, so no one else should give up on them. We had a very interesting discussion on how to handle physical pain. D and Z both said they tell their dentist not to give them Novocaine. They preferred to tolerate the pain. One inmate showed me his clavicle sticking out and said that it was never set properly during surgery so his range of motion would be affected for the rest of his life.

We settled into a meditation starting with the pranayama exercise. Moments later, following our class, B and D were waiting for me at the gate. I looked upward and saw more birds flying. The guys told me that they never noticed so many birds before I pointed them out at our previous walk down the courtyard. D asked about my book. I asked him if he would be willing to meet with me for an hour or two so he could provide me with some inside information about prison life. He seemed pleased that I thought of him and mentioned that perhaps his role could be "contributor." I stated that I liked the idea of having him write something because he could provide some information based on actual experience that I would not be privy to. I felt that his input would be valuable. I had two opportunities to tell D and the technical guy G that they had good energy. G said he felt like he had Divine intervention when he kept asking if he could work with the Chaplain in the chapel and the library. They both said they appreciated my uplifting heartfelt comments.

January 9, 2024

It was truly an amazing day! I arrived early and the inmates were late because they were quarantined. I learned that one of their fellow inmates fell ill the previous week and had to go to the infirmary. He never came back. The class size was small but it was absolutely perfect. We talked for about 15 minutes. I asked, "Does anyone know what happened with J?" Z said,

Doreena Durbin

"You mean the guy who was crawling under tables during one of our classes?" I responded "Yes." I said I missed him and hoped that he was ok. I was concerned that he might be getting bullied because of his sexual preference for men. I'm not here to judge. They said he had to be moved to another section of the prison because he threw a chair at someone in the chapel in the middle of a sermon.

There was one new guy so I briefly filled him in on meditation. I asked if he had ever experienced meditation before and he said, "Yes" he learned from a book. I told them that many people have used books to read about meditation; however, it is best to learn from a qualified teacher who can guide the meditator step-by-step into the state of meditation, where you do not have to keep track of time and think about what to do next. Taking a couple of minutes to come out of the meditation slowly is important so the nervous system doesn't get too stimulated. I explained that meditation is experiential, not intellectual. I told them that meditation will make them more aware of when they are focusing on the past or the future. The present moment is all there is. I told them one of the greatest benefits of meditation is to increase their awareness. I encouraged them to do it as often as they can. I informed them that one of the things I want to convey is how valuable they are. Their lives are not based on their deeds. We meditated for a full 20 minutes followed by the peaceful Gayatri Universal prayer. Afterwards, I read the English version, which I had put in my pocket that morning. I wanted them to understand the meaning of that beautiful Sanskrit prayer. After invoking the prayer, I felt the peace in the room resonating at a very high frequency and vibration. This prayer is often invoked for healing and deep relaxation and I had no doubts whatsoever, that it would be conducive for their healing.

Sanskrit Prayer English version:

O. God, Thou art the Giver of life, the remover of pains and sorrows, the Bestower of happiness. O. Creator of the Universe, may we receive thy supreme sin-destroying light.

May Thou guide our intellect in the right direction.

O. Lord! The Creator of the Universe, remove all forms of vice and sorrow from us, and give to us all Thy beneficial attributes.

O. Luminous God! Lead us to the noble path of thy devotion and grace; Lord! Thou knows all our deeds. Remove from us all our vices and sins. We offer in every way our homage and valuations to Thee.

O. Supreme Spirit! Lead us from untruth to truth, Lead us from darkness to light, Lead us from death to immortality.

O. Lord! In Thee may all be happy. May all be free from misery, may all realize goodness, and may no one suffer pain.

Peace; Peace; Peace.

I told them that I wanted them to find their most conducive time for meditation, because of all of the challenges and distractions, I could not advise them of the optimal time. Besides, I was not going to try to control their preferences or take away their free will. They needed to find the time and the space that is most conducive for them that would fit in their daily routine. With the support of their meditation and breathing practices, my hope is that they could learn to rise above their challenges while serving time in prison.

After the class I mentioned to D that I wanted to meet with the Reverend. He said he would walk with me to his office. The Reverend was happy to see me and gave me a hug. His beautiful energy was positive and uplifting. He said he heard about my classes from the inmates and asked me if I could teach him so he could also experience meditation. I told him I would be honored to teach him. He also mentioned there may be others joining us. Then D took me into the faith based dorms so I could see for myself a part of their prison experience—where they slept, watched TV, and hung out. I noticed that each large room was surrounded by walls of plexiglass so there was no privacy. There were about six dorms with 56 inmates per dorm or a total of 336 in each metal building. Standing in the corridor, you could see inside several dorms. The rooms were filled with bunk beds, chairs, and small tables. Inmates were spread out all around the rooms. Some were playing card games, some were reading, and others were watching TV. It was cramped. I saw for myself the lack of privacy and bright lights. I wondered how many of the inmates snored at night disturbing the other inmates. It was not very conducive for a quiet meditation, but with practice learning how to tune out the noise by focusing on the breath it may be possible to experience some moments of inner peace. I learned that the best times for quietness were in the early morning or late at night.

When I went outside to exit the courtyard, along the way I saw two inmates who were crouching with two beautiful healthy looking black cats. One was on the ground petting one of the cats. I asked them if the cats lived within the prison grounds. One of them identified himself as the "Catman." He said others called him that too. I asked if the inmates fed them scraps of food from their meals. He said a couple of guards fed them cat food and some inmates gave them food from the diner. I learned there were six cats who lived on the premises around the prison. He said that the cats were good therapy.

January 30, 2024

I arrived 1.5 hours early. The Chaplain wasn't there so I went to see the Reverend. I also met the other Chaplain from the Islam faith. I had an opportunity to speak with him prior to my class. We talked for about 15 minutes. He was very curious about meditation. I explained how it would not interfere with his Islamic faith.

The guys arrived about 15 minutes late but inmate R was sitting in the library waiting for the class to begin so we had an opportunity to chat. I told him that I wanted to hear his story. His long brown and gray beard was secured with two rubber bands. Following the class he said he enjoyed our chat. I did too. I found him to be a beautiful soul. Since the other guys were late, we had a chance to talk about the Catholic faith. He used to be a Protestant Christian but now he has decided to open up to Catholicism. He made the decision to open his vision to learn spiritual awakening practices like meditation and said he is enjoying learning from me. I asked him questions about how long he had been imprisoned and when he found the best time to meditate. He confessed that he sometimes meditates during the Christian services when he can just close his eyes and appear to be sleeping or praying. Two new men showed up. They were part of the Eastern based religion dorm and wanted to check out my group. They asked about meditation. He said in the Muslim faith they meditate with the attention on the breathing. Then Z showed up followed by the group of other inmates. After learning that he is 6'5" I asked him how he was able to sleep in the small cots that are in the dorms. He said since they don't have large beds, he has to get into a fetal position. I told D that I finished *Backward Beliefs,* which is the book that he recommended. I liked it. He then recommended Nanci Danison's book on manifestation entitled, *Create a New Reality.*

At the beginning of the class, I asked if there was anything they wanted to talk about. The group was very interactive. I asked B about Metta (loving kindness) meditation. He shared a great deal about sending loving kindness to friends as well as enemies including challenging people in his life. Two more guys shared that they also use a type of loving kindness meditation. I was pleased to see how easy and comfortable they were talking about sharing love and energy. We talked about how to use energy for healing and sending it to anyone anywhere in the world. I told them about how meditation can increase awareness and helps them "catch" themselves prior to losing control of their senses where they could easily react before making a mistake. Then D said that right before he came to the class he nearly got into a brawl with an inmate who pushed his buttons. His emotions of anger were raging. The other inmate had his fists in D's face. D was able to calm down quickly. Even though he was very angry, he was able to take a step back and view the incident with more awareness. After he calmed down, he was even able to energetically send the angry inmate compassion. I thought…that is real progress! He was able to let it go as he was taught to let go of thoughts during the state of meditation. J said that he came from a dysfunctional family where it was normal to go to prison. All of his close family members had served time. Three inmates said that it was also normal for everyone in his family as well. Jail was the norm in his neighborhood. Two other inmates said they are experiencing the same thing in their families. Some were living in gang infested neighborhoods. One of the 30- or 40- something white inmates covered with tattoos on his arms, neck, and face said he experienced the same thing. He had attended many of my classes and used to be a bit combative, while quoting scriptures. He defended Christianity when threatened by different beliefs that do not fit his religious ideology.

I told them how fortunate they are to have learned meditation, which will provide them with spiritual support. Based on my own experiences of practicing meditation for so many years, this powerful spiritual practice will make them feel that they have a greater sense of strength and have something to hold onto. Meditators often report that since they have learned how to get in touch with their inner beings through the practice of meditation, which is connected with the Creator or the One Source, that no matter what happens to them, everything will be ok. I told them that even though their physical bodies are confined, nothing can ever take away their spirits.

I find it very disheartening that when they are released from prison that many of them will return to the same environments that they left behind. They initially go to halfway houses that are not conducive to their wellbeing but at least they have a place to sleep. Fortunately, many of them will be going back into society with new coping skills. As they continue their meditation and spiritual practices like prayer and affirmations, their inner strength gets stronger especially after realizing their connection to the One Source. I encourage them to continue their meditation practices so they can help to heal their ancestral wounds and those that their families have endured for many generations.

Afterwards, we did a few rounds of pranayama, followed by a 20 minute meditation on the breath. My hope is that societies can be a source of hope and healing, so new spiritual energy can be infused and more programs such as this Prison Meditation Program will be available for incarcerated individuals when they integrate back to their communities. Hope and healing are very important for the offenders, their families, and the societies.

As we gathered in the library preparing to walk out, I was talking with several inmates when J came up behind me and gave me a hug. It was so natural that without thinking I did not avoid it so instead of stepping back, I patted him on the back just as I would have done with anyone who exuded positive energy. I was aware that the prison guards might not approve of the men touching a female during incarceration but I felt this instance was genuine and ok. I intuited that he was expressing gratitude like he might express to his mother. I noticed that since J has been coming to my classes, his energy has become more positive and gentle. Afterwards, I realized that J did not attend my first two classes where I informed the inmates that there would be no touching and I would be using the Namaste hand gesture pose. However, after teaching in the prison for over a year, I felt more relaxed since some of the inmates were vibrationally at a higher level. Besides, Covid was no longer a big issue, but I cannot be naive and too trusting. I still need to follow the rules. It is taboo to show this type of affection, especially for females in a men's prison. Therefore, I will try to be more cognizant and only shake their hands or give fist bumps.

One guy said he would not be coming to the next class because he was getting released in 12 days. We all clapped and wished him well. He has three daughters and was looking forward to beginning his new life with them. I asked for a show of hands on how many had daughters. Nearly all of them raised their hands. I told them how important they are in their daughters' lives and that they play a major role since they are influential in building their daughters' self esteem. It's important for girls to learn to have healthy relationships with men. It is important to tell them that they are loved but it's more important that they be respected. Of course, a father's love and guidance is just as important for their sons. Boys look for praise, not criticism. Any praise that is genuine will be remembered. I enjoyed the class very much and felt more comfortable than I had been at any other visit. My conversations with everyone were easy and free flowing. The guys were very receptive. The new inmate seemed a little reserved but it seemed like he was dealing with something personal. He was new to the penal system and I sensed that he was mentally processing what was happening to him. During meditation I noticed he was holding his head almost as if in beseeching prayer. D walked outside with me and said that I said something profound today. I said that meditation is experiential, whereas religion was more intellectual requiring interpretations and analysis of scriptures.

As I exited the building a large Hispanic man with a different uniform came out of the lobby at the same time. As we walked together to the parking lot I asked him what position he had at the prison. He said he is law enforcement for gangs. He had worked in various cities including Dallas and he was very familiar with areas where gang activity was taking place.

February 27, 2024

I arrived 45 minutes early. The patting down progress was the quickest I have ever experienced. I missed the shift changing of the guards. Two of the inmates were at the first gate and said they wanted to come to my class but they didn't get enough notice from the guards. I had an opportunity to speak with the Chaplain who was talking with three men who I learned were from South Korea. They were leading the Narc-Anon support group. The Chaplain was in his office so I stopped by to say hello. Only three guys showed up because several dorms where some inmates were housed were quarantined because of Covid. One or two of the inmates were diagnosed with Covid so they had to shut the entire dorms down. Z stopped by to bring me a note from D who was quarantined and apologized for not being able to attend my class. This is the first time D had missed any of my classes. He felt bad that he was not allowed out of the dorm to attend. The Chaplain popped his head in and apologized for the small number. I told him it was perfect and each of the three guys who showed up would get one-on-one training. It truly was perfect. Even if only one inmate showed up, that would have been fine too. I have learned to surrender to Divinity so I trusted that whatever happened was for a reason. I will continue to teach no matter what and I feel like I am blessed to have the opportunity to teach at this prison, so whoever showed up was perfectly fine with me. B was there. He had been to most of my classes and said he is able to meditate every day. He looked a little pale and tired and I was wondering if he might not be feeling well. Another guy, D, had been to several of my classes but I hadn't seen him for a while. The third guy came for the first time. He looked tough and was sporting several tattoos on his dark body. I introduced myself and welcomed him to the class. When he began speaking I became aware that there was something different about him. He shared that he is an empath and an intuitive and had some experience with meditation. We had a good conversation and I had the opportunity to get to know him. All three of the men were very spiritual so I was able to focus my class on them. DC said that coming to my class was a good birthday present. Today is his 32nd birthday. He said he is getting released in a few weeks. He thanked me for never talking about politics because the Christian faith based dorm was very right wing and there were a lot of fights because of political divisions. B also thanked me for offering the meditation program and said it was making a difference in his life. He was having insights and more awareness. The new inmate asked if he could invoke a Buddhist prayer. I approved. It was very nice and sounded familiar. I believe I had heard it previously at one of the Buddhist temples I had attended many years ago in Chicago during CPWR. When he finished I asked if they would like to hear the Universal Vedic Sanskrit Prayer. I invoked it, then when I finished, I noticed that all of them had their eyes closed. They said they enjoyed the peaceful feeling that permeated the room.

We started with two rounds of the pranayama, followed by a 20 minute meditation on the breath. We took several minutes to come out of the meditation. I intuited that the birthday guy was in the medical field so I asked him if that was true. He said he was a paramedic. I asked if he might be interested in going to medical school. He said that when he is released he planned to take care of his grandmother who was getting old and needed his help.

When we walked into the hallway to prepare to leave, we waited for a guard to unlock the gate. We chatted on the way to the next security gate. I asked if he was from Nigeria, which he was. He said that the majority of the guards were from Nigeria, and some from Kenya. I surprised him when I said goodbye in Nigerian.

I enjoy learning and speaking a little of various languages. He unlocked the gate and we continued chatting. The inmates were going to the diner for dinner. I asked if the food was good. They responded simultaneously, "No!"

As I was walking down the courtyard on my way to the parking lot, I passed several lines of inmates. Guards made them stop and wait for me to pass by. Many of the inmates smiled and others who knew me said they were coming to my next class. An African American inmate greeted me with the Namaste hand gesture. I was pleased and surprised by how many of the guys had attended previous classes. I greeted some of them by their first names. I recognized many of them who came to my classes.

March 5, 2024

Two inmates were at the security gate when I entered the courtyard. They said they were going to sign up for my class. When I walked into the library, G was standing in the hallway. I invited him in because I got the impression that he wanted to talk. He shared his story. Afterwards, I understood how he wound up in prison. He had no role models in his life and no memory of his mother. When he was five years old, he recalls meeting his father who informed him that it was the last time he would see him. He was right. He never saw his father again. He was sent to multiple foster homes and he kept running away in the hopes of being returned to his father. No one ever explained to him what happened to his dad. I sensed that the foster care system had failed him.

I had called the Chaplain on March 4 to see if the guys in Dorm #3 were released from quarantine. He said he could make that happen since a week was sufficient to release them from quarantine following an incident of Covid in the dorm. I was pleased to see that they all showed up for class. Once they settled in I told them I was curious as to why I have never heard them curse, which I thought would have been normal, especially in a men's prison. I wondered if they got punished by guards if they were overheard cursing. Z spoke up and said it was out of respect for me since I am a woman. I said that I appreciated that and thanked them.

Prior to starting meditation I asked them if they would like to meditate on the breath or a mantra. Some said the mantra but the majority of them did not specify so I told them that we would use the breath since there were new guys who might forget the mantra if they tried to have future meditations. Being able to meditate on the breath is beneficial and they would be able to use it for the rest of their lives, where you do not have to recall the mantra. I spoke about a friend from AMS who had taught meditation in a women's prison in Illinois. She said that all of them who meditated regularly got an early release. I believe this gave the inmates an incentive to continue. I spoke about how our energy and vibration changes with regularity of practicing meditation. It has been obvious to me that those who have been attending my classes for the past year have become less tense, their faces appear softer, and their eyes are brighter. I am often amazed at their spiritual development. I asked if there was anything they would like to talk about. One of the new guys said he was Catholic and he is often treated with contempt for not being a Protestant. I said that Jesus was inclusive to everyone and did not discriminate, nor did he look for revenge following the abuse he suffered. He would not exclude anyone. He taught by example. They told me that one of the volunteers in the faith based dorm said they were shown a sign to beware of anything that had words like yoga, meditation, tarot, Islam, Wicca, or paganism. Some of the inmates were upset and said they are uneducated because meditation is part of their spiritual practices. Z, a practitioner of Islam was upset that they would put Islam into that objectionable category because Muslims believe in Jesus. He said they are evidently uneducated. We all had a good interactive conversation. We started with a couple of rounds of pranayama, followed by a 20 minute meditation. There was a sense of Oneness in the room.

As we were standing in the hallway preparing to walk outside, Z expressed that I am just like a woman who changes her mind like other women in his life. He was looking forward to meditating on the mantra. Then when I switched to the breathing he was disappointed. I promised him that we would meditate using the mantra at our next class. A guard from Nigeria who came to unlock the door so we could begin our walk down the courtyard was very friendly with me and the inmates. I thought he seemed like a different, more compassionate kind of man. I wondered if he was sensing the higher vibrations that the inmates were emanating.

March 26, 2024

I brought new fliers to have posted in several dorms. At our previous class, D offered a few suggestions that might motivate some of the guys who were more focused on the body to come to our class. He said they worked out a lot to become more buff. I liked his suggestions and decided to incorporate them on my next flier by changing the picture and some of the text.

I arrived early. I saw the Reverend on the way to the library. He was planning to visit me to inquire if I would come to his philanthropy organization to teach him and his colleagues how to meditate. I gladly accepted hoping to continue spreading spiritual and intellectual knowledge about meditation. The Chaplain greeted me with a smile and a handshake. I chatted with the Chaplain from the Muslim based group, a few volunteers, and some inmates. I really enjoy coming to teach and share good cheer. I feel like I'm part of the prison family.

My regulars showed up, D, Z, B, R, J, J. I looked around the room and was struck by this beautiful group of spiritual men who sat in front of me. Members of society might view them in

143

an unfavorable way but I don't. They are like anyone else. I see them as spiritual brothers, sons, and cousins. Per my promise to Z, we began with the mantra meditation. One new inmate who is a Life Couch joined us to see what I was teaching so he could encourage other inmates to come. I was delighted that B brought his writing for the book. D had given me his weeks ago. Two other inmates wanted to write something as well and said they would bring them to the next class. It was truly heartwarming to see the inmates! I felt a sense of warmth and peace emanating from them. I am more aware of the Divinity that resides within them as they light up the prison with their beautiful presence. Like lotus flowers in the mud, they were growing into beautiful spiritual beings. I loved the way R shared his thoughts so beautifully. He shared how he feels different since he's been coming to the meditation classes. I noticed D getting a bit emotional because of R's beautiful sharing. I love the way our classes are deepening as they are free to express their emotions. I notice more love and compassion flowing through everyone. We started with a check in to see how everyone was doing and if the recent lockdown had been difficult for them.

We talked about the visualization practice. I read a page of a transcript that Gururaj gave at a Chicago prison. Then I led them into a round of pranayama. Z spoke about his experiences. I appreciate his valuable input in the classes as he shares elements of his Muslim faith with the class.

Before leaving, I decided to speak with the Chaplain about the April 9 date for the next class. I mistakenly thought that the Solar Eclipse was happening on that same day and I did not want to miss it. It did not interfere because it occurred on April 8 so I stayed home and watched it in my backyard.

Get an Inner Life! MEDITATE

Experience Freedom and Peace of Mind through the Power of Meditation

WHAT IS MEDITATION? Meditation is an inward journey and has been practiced for thousands of years in various forms by people of many different faiths and backgrounds. Focusing the mind on the breath, a mantra or an activity can increase awareness and achieve a mentally clear and emotionally calm and stable mind.

- Meditation is not a religion and is not exclusive to any religion.
- Learn the difference between meditation and prayer.
- The goal of meditation is to achieve an inner state of peace and awareness.

Freedom is Found Within

Learn how to quiet the mind by focusing on the breath to find peace. Meditation is simple and easy to do. No special postures are required.

- Learn how to tap into the same powers and mental stamina that elite high Performance, pro athletes and multimillionaires use

In basketball - as in life - true joy comes from being fully present in each and every moment.
Phil Jackson, Chicago Bulls NBA Coach

- Combat depression
- Tame the Ego Mind
- Increase Focus and Concentration

March 26, April 9, April 23, May 7, 2024

Where: [ ] State Prison - Chapel

Time: 3:00 - 4:30 pm

Instructor: Doreena

* Note to Inmates: For enrollment, you must send an I-60 to Chaplaincy.

I asked D and the guard if they could walk with me to the gate into the courtyard. After a short distance we parted ways. One of the inmates saw me in the courtyard and said he heard about my class so we chatted for a few minutes. He was a boxer on the outside and didn't know if it would be a good fit for him. D showed him my new flier with the tattooed meditating man and the new text. He came to the next class.

April 9, 2024

Very fun interesting day! One of the security guards was very friendly when I walked in from the parking lot. BB and two other inmates were waiting by the last gate for a guard to unlock it so they could come to my class. The guys from the faith based dorm arrived 15 minutes later. One of the guys asked me if I needed a candle to teach the visualization meditation practice. I responded "Yes!" One of the inmates had access to the chapel where it was stored for the priest to use for the Catholic ceremonies. He brought it into the library. There was lots of bantering, joking, and surprised looks as I was asking if any of them had a lighter or a match to light the candle. Of course I knew that lighters or matches were prohibited but I thought that since a guard would be present outside to the library and it would be used for spiritual teaching purposes perhaps they could make an exception like they do for the priests. As I walked into the Chaplain's office to say hello, he was talking with the Reverend. I showed them the candle and informed them it was for teaching a visualization practice for focusing. The inmates were eager to learn this new meditation practice. The inmates were standing close behind me waiting to hear their responses. I got the sense that they knew what the response would be. With raised voices and in unison, the Chaplain and the Reverend both shouted, "No"! When we closed the door, their emphatic and immediate responses evoked chuckling from me and the inmates. I felt like we were siblings trying to get away with something. I told the inmates that we would figure it out. One of them suggested that I get a battery operated candle from a Dollar Store. I thought that was a good idea so I said that I would look into it and try to bring it to our next class.

The guys followed me into the library to begin the breathing practice. I asked B to demonstrate to the other guys how to take a deep breath on the count of 4, hold the breath for a count of 16 and exhale on the count of 8. When done properly, the stomach muscles should expand and contract during the breathing practice. I counted as B demonstrated. We started with a few rounds of pranayama followed by a 20 minute mantra meditation. One of the guys asked if I know how to do Reiki. He had heard that it was helpful for people who are suffering from physical disorders. Another one asked if I would send them healing energy during the meditation. When we finished, D wanted to know if I had sent healing energy throughout the meditation. He had an abscessed tooth and was in a lot of pain. He said that I must have because the pain was gone before the meditation ended. He wanted to know if I had anything to do with that. I admitted that I invoked healing energy during the meditation. I spoke about how powerful group prayer and healing energy can be. I explained that the healer just acts as an open channel, like a hollow flute, and without ego. The healer is just a channel as they invoke a higher power, which clears the channel for energy to pass through. I have learned that energy healers should never take credit for healings because they are not doing anything except allowing energy to flow through unobstructed. The ego should never be involved.

One the new guys shared that he had lost a niece by suicide and was grieving her loss. We had a very spiritual conversation about near death experiences, seeing entities, or feeling a presence. Questions about the afterlife and a very interesting discussion ensued.

April 23, 2024

There were a few older men in the room across from the library near the Chaplain's office. I learned that they were volunteers. I went to say hello to the Chaplain. I like his energy. He is a wonderful, good natured, spiritual man and I like our rapport. He has great energy and generally portrays a smiling face, unless I show up late. Today he was happy and smiling.

The guys entered the library and seemed excited about the candle technique. They remembered at the previous class, I told them that I was going to bring a battery operated candle to teach them tratak. I asked one of the guys to get the candle holder while I installed a battery for the candle, which I found on Amazon. I tried the smaller candle at the Dollar Store but when I tested it, I did not get an after image. The larger candle looked real and was perfect! However, I needed to make sure it worked as a substitute for a real candle. I was pleased to see the boxer in the room. I met him in the courtyard after the previous class. He said he had heard about my class and wanted to check it out. I welcomed him. The inmates all introduced themselves. I asked the guys to arrange the chairs to be positioned in a semicircle so everyone could have an eye level view of the fake candle flame. During instruction, I sat in the middle chair between Z and D and felt very centered, and spoke clearly and deliberately as I described the benefits and purpose of the tratak meditation. I sensed they were eager to learn this new visualization technique. I understood why I was not allowed to use a lighter or match. A few moments later the Chaplain popped his head in and I showed him the battery operated candle. He gave me a thumbs up and a nod. We settled in and I taught them how to observe the candle "flame," as I explained how to just allow thoughts to come and go as they were taught to do in our other meditations. As in those meditation practices, they are taught to put their attention on their breathing or a mantra. Most of the ceiling lights were turned off. I instructed them step-by-step to gaze at the candle flame effortlessly for several minutes. After a few minutes, I asked them to close their eyes and put their attention on the space between their eyebrows, otherwise known as the third eye (ajna chakra) and let me know if they got an afterimage of the candle flame. They all raised their hands. I was very pleased that this method would work in the prison environment. They observed the candle flame for a second time for several minutes. Then closed their eyes to observe the after image of the flame. After several minutes of observing the flame, I instructed them to raise their hand if they got an after image.

Once again, they all raised their hands. I was happy to know that the battery operated fake candle was working. Now they could practice this technique with a real candle after their release back to the real world. We ended with two rounds of pranayama.

Afterwards, the group was interactive and asked questions after I spoke about the flow experience as described by Mihaly Csikszentmihalyi in his book entitled, "Flow: The Psychology of Optimal Experience." The book describes how some athletes improve the quality of their lives by controlling a heightened state of consciousness. For the inmates who were involved in sports, especially the boxer who was attending today's class, I shared the experience I had with Muhammed Ali, at Chicago's O'Hare airport in the 70's. I wanted them to let them know that meditation was not for cowards. It is sometimes called the hero's path since it transcends the physical realm and involves an exploration of the inner self. I explained that airport security was not as strict during the 70's. I told them that I was picking up a friend late one evening and happened to walk by one of the areas where a few people were waiting for passengers to debark. As I walked by, I noticed the American professional boxer, Muhammed Ali demonstrating boxing punches to a couple of men. I must have caught his attention with my long dark hair and red long sleeve mini dress because he stopped in the middle of showing punches and began conversing with me. After our conversation, he asked me if I would like to join him and some of his friends at a condo in downtown Chicago for a little gathering. I told him that I could not because I was picking up a friend who was flying in from New York. He wrote down his phone number and the address on a piece of paper in the event I could join him.

I also told them about Phil Jackson who was a former NBA basketball player and coach for the Chicago Bulls. He helped his team by teaching them Zen meditation and mindfulness, which he explained helped build mental strength and encouraged teamwork. He taught his players including Michael Jordan, Scottie Pippin, and Dennis Rodman how to meditate using Zen practices. This amazing coach brought the Bulls through six championships.[9]

Great interactive class!

May 7, 2024

I felt like today was significant, perhaps because I knew that I would be moving soon because I can't take the Texas heat. It was already 94 degrees and I knew it would only get hotter as summer was fast approaching. My body gets drained and weakened in hot weather and I did not want to pass out from heat stroke in the prison courtyard. They have a medical facility for the inmates but if I suffer an illness or accident, I would be taken by paramedics to a local hospital. The Chaplain and I talked a little and I shared that May would probably be my last month because I would be moving. I am certainly not fond of the 100 degree and higher temperatures, the snakes, and the huge spiders!

I wanted to give the inmates as much information as I could. The word must have gotten around about the last class because several new guys showed up, including the boxer from the last class. One of the new inmates was waiting for me outside of the library. I invited him to sit inside so I could get to know him before the other guys showed up. DH was a nice African American man, who had great energy. I sensed he was different. While we were waiting for the other inmates, he shared his story with me and how he got into prison. He was very educated. He was eager to learn about meditation and had good questions. I understood the other inmates were being detained for a short while in their dorms due to an altercation or a prison check. That gave me and DH a chance to talk about the questions he had about meditation. When the other guys arrived, they settled in very quickly and I shared that I would only be coming for one or two more classes because I was planning to move out of state. I conveyed that this book would serve as a reminder for all of the teachings and discussions that we've had in our classes during 2023 and

2024. I hoped they would continue their meditation practices and incorporate the teachings into their lives.

I told them about when I taught some ex-convicts meditation, I also helped them prepare for jobs when they are released. I wanted them to pay attention to their body language when presenting for job interviews. I noticed light was shining from R's eyes. I have seen a positive change in him since he has been practicing meditation. He told me he was testing meditation so he could experience the benefits. I told the guys how much I enjoy coming to the prison to teach them. We had a nice interactive class.

We started with pranayama then settled into a meditation on the breath. D inquired about the rhythm of the 4:16:8. He had a difficult time holding his breath for 16 seconds. I said that he could speed up the rhythm, however, it is important to keep the same pace. I guided them into the meditation. A beautiful peaceful energy filled the room. Afterwards, I read a couple of paragraphs from Gururaj's talk at Lorton Prison in Virginia. A good discussion ensued.

I told them how to pay attention to adrenaline rushes when they would get emotionally triggered and to use their breathing to calm down. I asked if anyone wanted to share with the new guys how this worked for them when they were around people who pushed their buttons. Two of them expressed their experiences and how it helped them to calm down quickly.

I felt like the Pied Piper as I led the inmates out of the door through the last the security gate into the courtyard. G was holding the gate for me to pass through. A guard shouted at him and told him step aside so I could enter first. I responded that he is ok and that he was in my class and was holding the door for me in a gentlemanly fashion. Whenever I walk down the courtyard, it is customary for all of the inmates step aside to allow me to go first. As the boxer said goodbye he looked at me and gestured "I got you" as he pointed with two fingers from his eyes to my eyes and verbalized, "You're deep." I sensed that he was talking about the topics I spoke about during our class. I witnessed another guard further down the courtyard shouting at inmates. I continued walking and saw some of them going to the diner for dinner. I walked the rest of the way alone feeling exuberant as I passed by at least 60 inmates who were acknowledging me with nods and smiles, as they verbalized, "Stay safe." The female officers in the front lobby were extra friendly. When I went outside, it was Guard Appreciation Day and ribs were cooking outside in a huge pit. I smelled them and decided that I must break my "no beef, no pork" diet at least once before moving from Texas and eat some ribs. I will say a prayer and bless the meat!

May 21, 2024 (was supposed to be my last class)

Today was the largest class. The library was filled to capacity. I was pleased. Two new guys introduced themselves. They were waiting at the gate for me to arrive so the guard could unlock the gate. One was a Muslim and had heard about the class from one of the other Muslim participants. We had a chance to introduce ourselves before the room began filling up.

I learned that B, the young man who practices Metta (loving kindness) got transferred to a better, more flexible unit. I am happy for him, however, I will miss him since he always had a beautiful peaceful presence in our classes. I wish I could have said goodbye and wished him well before my last day. Hopefully he will read this book and know I appreciated his presence during our classes.

D asked how meditation can help with addictions. Many of the guys are imprisoned due to issues involving alcohol and drugs so I thought those were important topics of discussion. D always has great ideas, which I have often utilized. We focused the class on addictions. After my talk one of the guys who had attended Alcoholics Anonymous classes said that I said the same things they are taught, which included: Meditate to connect with a higher power, pay attention to subtle body triggers, face your demons with courage, don't be afraid to ask for help, and make amends to people you may have hurt or offended while under the influence. Look ahead and consider the consequences when you have the desire to imbibe or do drugs. Continue your meditation practices and (most importantly) do the 4:16:8 breathing practice, which helps to clear out toxins in your body.

June 4, 2024

I was asked to come today even though May 21 was supposed to be my last class. The inmates are benefitting from my classes, and have asked me to continue my program until I find a replacement. I feel like I'm part of the large family as I continue to hear their stories of how and why they are serving time. We all find camaraderie and a desire to experience the peaceful library with an air conditioner and a small fan. A great group of guys and a few new inmates showed up. One was wearing a yarmulke, and another guy was a practitioner of Transcendental Meditation (™). I enjoyed meeting them and seeing the regulars who seemed to be in good spirits as we conversed with each other.

A female guard whom I had never met before had the key to open the gate. She was very surprised that the gate opened easily. She said that she had struggled with it many times so I must be carrying good energy and asked if I could pass some on to her. She asked what I was teaching and said that she could probably benefit from my program. I invited her to attend one of my classes; however, I knew she was on the job so it would not happen. While waiting for the inmates, G came into the library to talk. He shared a notebook of journaling and writings. Another inmate entered and G left to carry on his prison role of assisting the Chaplain. The guard asked the other inmate to leave. I learned that inmates could not be left alone with me without a guard present. I did not question the authority and rules and regulations so he left temporarily until the other guys began filing in one after the other.

We shared small talk for a few minutes about how much longer I could continue my program. We spoke about various types of meditation for the new guys and the idea of "letting go" of thoughts during the meditative state. I explained how it helps to set the stage for letting go of things in our lives that have caused hurt and pain, such as people who have said hurtful things to us that we are still holding onto. We settled into a mantra meditation. It was a very peaceful meditation and I felt positive energy permeate throughout the room. When we came out, the inmate who traveled around the world during his military service asked if we could continue with another meditation instead of talking because he loved the peace and silence. He referred to me as a Guru and liked the way I led them into the meditative state. One of the guys asked if we could chant together like we did in one of our previous classes. Before we began, I spoke about vibrations of sounds and how it is best to use sounds for their vibratory value, instead of using words which would invite thoughts to enter the mind. We talked about the Sanskrit language. We talked about how chants are used in the various religious traditions such as Muslim, Buddhist, and Hindu chants. One guy said he was from the Comanche Native American tribe and asked if he could say a bit of their chant. He had practiced Transcendental Meditation and asked if he could invoke the Gayatri mantra. I had learned this powerful Sanskrit mantra many years ago so I was very familiar with it. It is said to be one of the oldest and most powerful mantras. It was written during the Vedic period (1500-500 BCE) and has been claimed to contain all of the knowledge of the Universe. He shared a portion of the prayer that he knew then I finished the rest of it. The guys said they could feel the peaceful energies that was in the room. When I finished the last two-thirds of the Sanskrit prayer, R said he could feel his entire body resonating with the peaceful energies. One of the guys asked if we could do the chant that begins with "Aim hrim crim"... I wrote it on the white board and we chanted together. I also wrote the five senses on the white boards and told them how we get sensory input from our environment. I spoke about the three layers of the mind, beginning with the conscious level of the mind, the subconscious level, where impressions and memories are stored, then the superconscious level, which is our spiritual connection with Divinity.

After class, we gathered in the hallway to wait for a guard who was going to unlock the security gate. Some inmates from the Catholic faith based dorm were coming out of the chapel so I had the opportunity to talk with them. The Reverend was in the courtyard so we had a chance to talk for a few minutes.

June 18, 2024

I arrived about 45 minutes early and found the Eastern religion based volunteer waiting for me in the lobby. I learned that he is the only male volunteer in Texas who teaches a Buddhist based meditation practice in prisons. He told me that I am the only female who teaches meditation at prisons in the state of Texas. However, my program is not based on any religion. Instead, it encompasses all religions and paradoxically, no religion. The Chaplain suggested that he get my permission to come to my class so he called me while I was driving to inquire if I approved.

The inmates had a prison check in their dorms so the class would be starting late. When the inmates arrived, extra chairs needed to be brought in. I introduced our guest even though several of the inmates had attended his classes and already knew him. He spoke for a bit then I was ready to begin my class so I allowed him to finish then I stated that since it is my class that I would do most of the talking. I was happy to see Z who missed the last few classes due to a conflict with another class he had been attending.

Doreena Durbin

I'm sure the guys were happy to get into an air-conditioned room out of the 95 degree heat. I learned that C would be released tomorrow and I wished him well.

I asked them if they would like me to read a page from my book, which I had printed out. Interestingly, we began the class speaking about chants and prayers. The page I read weaved perfectly with our topic on chants. I wrote the chant on the whiteboard and explained the benefit of doing chants, which would raise the vibrations in the room. We followed with 20 minutes of the mantra meditation. DH and the volunteer immersed themselves in their inner peace and did not come out of the meditation for about 30 minutes. The rest of the guys shared their experiences. One of the guys spoke about synchronicity and how things lined up for him since he's been meditating. I spoke about healing and how grateful I am to have met all of them. How I feel that they were teaching me as much as I had taught them. I held back tears of love and emotion. I feel that they have made me a better teacher. I felt validated and heard.

As we were walking through the courtyard, one of the inmates showed me a bird's nest that had eggs in it. He said it was a yellow bird who showed up for the second year in a row, to build a nest on top of a pole next to an security gate in the courtyard. It was a very unusual spot but the bird chose that small space for a reason. I knew that the strategic unlikely location it chose was significant because the inmates recalled our conversation about "the birds." I thought it would bring a little reflection and joy from the outside world into some of the inmates' lives. I wanted to stop and see if the Reverend was in his office so I could say goodbye, but there was no need because he showed up in the courtyard to give me a final hug and to tell me how much he and the inmates appreciated my service. I was very happy to see him to provide him with an acknowledgement for helping me get my program launched in the prison.

July 2, 2024

I decided to have more classes since I my move was delayed. When I arrived it was 100 degrees. When I left a few hours later, it was 106! This was the first time that I was in the courtyard alone with no one outside; not even the guards ventured out. I felt like I was in the Twilight Zone. I caught a brief glimpse of the Warden who entered a building. The walk was brutal and the sun showed no mercy. I supposed everyone was staying inside where there were big fans, which circulated hot air. I hoped the Chaplain was waiting at the last gate to let me in. He was. We sat down for a few minutes to talk about my replacement who changed his mind because of conflicts with his family life. I had planned on bringing him so I could introduce him and see the guys one last time. I was informed that they were jubilant when they found out I was coming! The Chaplain asked if he could put me on the schedule to teach July 16. I agreed as long as I was not in the process of moving. I was looking forward to seeing who would show up in my class. Two inmates were already in the library. Others began coming in until nearly every chair was filled. There were a few new guys who showed up. I waited for my inner prompt to see what today's class topic would be after I had the opportunity to sense the room. The world "attachment" popped in my head. I spoke briefly about the kinds of attachments we have: attachments to people, places, food, even the bunks where they are lay their heads at night.

I wanted to do something special for them today, especially since it might be my last class. I had been thinking about it for weeks but I just needed to make sure it was the time where there were no interruptions. I had picked up a bottle of water that was in an ice chest before leaving the front lobby. We small talked a little to allow time for everyone who was coming to show up and settle in. Then I guided them into a meditation focusing on the breath. After 20 minutes I told them to continue with their eyes closed and that I was going to go around the room and perform a healing exercise, which is similar to an initiation. I dipped my fingers into the bottle cap of water and touched their foreheads in the third eye area while channeling healing energy. Holy water and ashes are often used in many similar ceremonies. Using the bottle cap, I filled it several times, as I went to each and every inmate in my class.

Afterwards, the guys seemed very peaceful and appreciative. Many of them thanked me for caring enough about them to drive an hour and a half in scorching hot weather to offer my class, and take the half mile walk in the courtyard to provide them with meditation and healing. I told them how important it is to seek balance in life. One of the guys talked about Yin & Yang. I added how walking meditation is done and how my Buddhist monk friend used to teach it while saying…rising…falling. When one foot goes up, the other foot goes down. There is a middle point between the two.

D asked a question about empaths and wanted me to describe the experience. I told them that living life as an intuitive empath, which is closely aligned with high sensitivity, can be both a blessing and a curse. Intuition is very strong but feeling negative energy on an object in resale or antique shops can sometimes feel energetically draining, especially when it was previously owned or worn by someone who might have emanated intense negative angry energy. It carries an impression of that person, who might have owned certain objects, including jewelry, clothing, or household objects. One of the guys wanted to know if I ever fished and if so, how would I bait the hook using worms? I said I have fished before but I would never bait the hook! The only time I fished, after catching them, I put them back in their habitat. I noticed some smiles. I thought that fish also deserve freedom! I am aware of nature's way of the continuation of life for the benefit of the people in society, but I don't want to be the hunter or killer of other life forms to sustain myself.

After class, D said he had something in his dorm that might direct me to finding a replacement for my prison meditation program.

I walked with him towards the dorm and he asked if I wanted to come in to get a sense of the hot conditions in their dorms. It was too hot to wait outside in the sun so I agreed. The first thing I noticed were two large fans. The inmates were in various stages of undress. The majority were shirtless. Z and J saw me from the dorm adjacent to D's. They both came out to greet me. J gave me a big hug. I didn't deny him even though other inmates could see from the full length see-through plexiglass walls. I always have the sense that I am a mother figure to him ever since he shared with me that he lost his mom just a week prior to meeting him.

Based on his story I got the feeling that he grew up in a Black impoverished community.

(See his story, titled *The Book*). I love his sweet pure energy.

I didn't stay inside the dorm for more than 5-10 minutes because I did not want to invade their privacy but it was good to see J and Z!

July 16, 2024

When the temperature rose to 110 degrees, I asked the inmates how they were able to tolerate the heat, especially since their dorms are located in metal buildings. D responded and said that he has learned to acclimate his body to the heat. Coming from Chicago, I am used to cold winters and hot, humid summers. I learned something that day and opened up to the experiences of inmates who have lived their lives in heat that I often find intolerable—especially with the prison rules for female volunteers who are supposed to cover up from neck to toe and not wear white.

Several new guys were in the class. We small talked for about 10 minutes until the other guys showed up. I decided to speak a little about attachments. D shared that he was getting out in two weeks. July 30 could be both of our last day. I asked him if he was excited about getting out. I was surprised when he said, "No!"

He said he is content and has learned to "rise above" the prison experience. He was getting lots of sleep and doesn't have a job so he is content.

I brought the brass chimes and demonstrated that when the meditation was ending they would hear it ring and to come out of the meditation gradually not abruptly.

One of the Hispanic Navy veterans shared an issue he had with one of the employees in the infirmary. He had suffered an ear injury and could not hear one of the commands that the guard was shouting. He did not appreciate being disrespected since he had served our country honorably.

R appeared a little reserved and melancholic. I reached out to him by email and offered to send him love, light, and healing.

Walking out, D gave me a nice hug in the event I will not see him again. However, it is possible that I might see him in two weeks on his last day because it might also be my last day. He had attended all of my classes.

July 30, 2024

When I arrived I announced to the Chaplain and the inmates that today is officially my last day for my classes. I can no longer take the heat. They didn't believe me because they have heard me say that before. They tried to convince me that summer is almost over and that I should stay. I got dizzy walking down the courtyard in the 100 degree temperature and thought I was going to lose my balance and pass out. I had heat stroke a number of times so I know the signs. I needed water but the ice chest in the lobby was empty. As I walked outside, one of the female officers noticed I was wobbly and was having difficulty keeping my balance. She asked if I was ok. I was not. When I said I needed water, she asked a guard to take me inside and give me a bottle of cold water. I was grateful but I wondered how the inmates were handling the heat inside of their metal dorms. I also wondered if they have free access to water. Needless to say, I was very concerned about their wellbeing as well as my own.

A few inmates were already waiting then my regulars began showing up including: R, J, Z, and others. There were a few new guys. D had been released and was sent to a half way house. I felt an energetic gap without his spiritual presence. An older African American gentleman did not know what to expect from my class but said he was led by a higher power. I started talking about D telling us at a previous class that he was content in prison. I asked if any of them are able to find any positives in prison. None of them felt a sense of contentment. When the class began, the new inmate began to smile. His eyes lit up when I began speaking about the power of meditation and aligning with Universal energy. He came from a Christian background and said he felt like an energetic force drew him into the library. Another new guy was familiar with Metta meditation. I welcomed them both. We started the class with a brief body scan followed by a few rounds of breathing, then a 20 minute meditation using the mantra. Questions were asked and I expounded on topics including the benefits of meditation, anger, the ego, adrenaline rushes, perception and other subjects as one flowed into another. One of the regular guys who had attended many of the classes shared that he had an experience during meditation that was similar to lucid dreaming.

While preparing to leave the guys came up to thank me one by one with handshakes and hugs. It felt good to let my guard down a bit to acknowledge them with hugs. The Chaplain teased and said he was going to lock me in so I couldn't leave, so I would continue my classes. I ran into the Reverend in the courtyard and had an opportunity to chat for a few minutes.

Even though my heart wants to continue I feel that I will jeopardize my own wellbeing by continuing. I felt that I needed to shift my

Doreena Durbin

attention by helping inmates and prisons on a larger scale by getting my book published and writing letters to government officials to provide air conditioners. I was angry that the inmates were being treated inhumanely. When I got in my car for the drive home, my intuitive lightbulb went on and I tuned into NPR radio. I immediately heard a news story on NPR news about a lawsuit that was currently in progress that Texas prisons were treating the inmates inhumanly by not installing air conditioners in the prisons. I learned that many inmates had suffered heat stroke due to lack of air conditioners. The prisons were being sued for cruel and unusual punishment.

162

CHAPTER 17

MEETING A SPIRITUAL MASTER

In 1977 an unforeseen spiritual force drew me to Lake Havasu, Arizona to attend my first meditation retreat. I had no expectations and felt a sense of curiosity and wonder about what would unfold during the next five days. A fully realized Spiritual Master from India walked into the room wearing a shiny brown jacket with a Nehru collar and matching brown pants. It nearly matched his skin tone. I was struck by the golden aura that surrounded him. I looked around to see if a yellow light was shining on him but there was not. His energy field was palpable and I felt waves of love and light emanating from him. Gururaj Ananda Yogi traveled from South Africa to spend five glorious days with us. He said he enjoyed driving through the Arizona desert and that everything was bathed in gold. His ancient spiritual practices were so profound and life changing. I was looking for peace and a way to handle the stress in my life while raising an infant son and a four year old daughter when I was working as a musician in Las Vegas. I was mesmerized when Gururaj started speaking about the Big Bang, God, and the Universe. As he spoke, I saw sparks of light surrounding him. I felt like I was time traveling through the cosmos. I also felt like I had known him for lifetimes. There was something very ancient about him. I had been meditating twice a day for a year with his individual spiritual practices and was receiving tremendous physical, mental, and spiritual benefits. I noticed an expansion in my awareness and a drop in my stress levels. I was experiencing a sense of excitement because I found something that would help me on my life path. It was working! I had gone to at least a hundred churches and religious institutions in the various states where I had lived, but I never heard anyone speak about the things he was expounding upon. He was wise and reached the depths of my soul. He shared his knowledge and spirit with everyone who attended the retreat. I was struck by his profound wisdom and his ability to combine science and spirituality, which later became my passion in understanding the world around me. Here was a live teacher who showed up in my life at the time I was dealing with a tremendous amount of stress. I needed to be assured that everything was going to be ok.

***

Gururaj gave the following satsangs at prisons. Satsang is the term used when a spiritual master speaks at a gathering of truth seekers. The following is a portion of two of his satsangs.

GURURAJ PRISON SATSANGS
Chicago, IL (1980)

So rememberings of the past is not the answer. That leads to greater misery and it leads to guilt. But analysis of the past means that we are trying to understand the past. We try to understand the motivation, what made us perform such an action. And if you find that you are forced into certain circumstances, which ninety-nine percent of all actions would prove, then you do not need to feel guilty about it. I was invited to one of the biggest prisons near Chicago to give a talk last year. And as a matter of fact we have a prisons' program going on in America for rehabilitation of the prisoners. Because a prison is not somewhere where you punish someone. A prison is a place where you rehabilitate someone. So we introduced this program in this, one of the largest in America I believe and of course, from there it is spreading to various other States. So I told those prisoners there, "You are in prison, why are you in prison? You might have been a rapist. You might have murdered someone. You might have stolen. You might have done one of so, so many things. Why did you do it? It could have been due to many reasons. Firstly, force of circumstance. Secondly through an imbalanced mind, where at that time you could not discriminate between right and wrong. And all your actions were regarded to be anti-social because of the social norms society has put upon us. But does that make you a bad person? You are judged by society to be bad, but are you really bad. No. The spirit within you is forever Divine and forever good. So do not think of the actions you have done in the past. Better thing to do is repentance and repentance itself has analysis built into it, to try and find the cause. And when you find the cause, the guilt would disappear."

So sometimes it is a fallacy to say that how can we learn from the past to build a future? Yes, you can. But it would become fallacious if you just remember the past. Then you cannot build upon it. For who is a sinner? You are not a sinner. You never have been a sinner. Only society brands you to be a sinner. But in God's eyes are you a sinner? Do you think that God's Grace would fall equally upon those that are regarded to be bad and those that are regarded to be good? If you were a sinner, then Divinity would discard you. But in His eyes no one is a sinner. Everyone is equal but it is your mind conditioned by society, that makes you a sinner. And because everyone around you, right from the time you were born and started getting some understanding, your parents forced upon you, 'Don't do this and don't do that and don't do that.' Then you go to school and the teachers 'Don't, don't, don't do this and don't do that and that and that and that.' And then you grow up more and you mix with adults and they all have their particular norms. Something could be a sin in one country while it would not be a sin in another country.

These are all moral laws and all morality is made by man and not by God. The thing to think about is purity, not morality. Are you going to go on - my ideas might be very revolutionary but it is within the norms of Gods laws - are you going to live your life according to man's law or God's law? That is the question one must ask himself. So going back into the past and remembering it and feeling guilty and miserable, that is not the way of progress. The way of progress is to say, "Okay, I have done this. Why did I do it and if I find that person in my mind, if I find that I have done something wrong then I would pray, meditate, become in a peaceful quiet state of mind and then pray sincerely, Lord forgive me, for I did not know what I did." Did Christ not say that on the cross, "Forgive them Father, they know not what they do"? You say that to yourself. You ask the Father the same thing. "Forgive me Father, I did not know what I do." For if you knew what you did, you would have not done it. It was a mental perversion, a kind of madness that made you perform an act which is anti-social or if not anti-social then harmful to others and harmful to yourself. Always remember one thing that when you harm someone else, you're harming yourself more. Because you will always remember that and there is the torture, there is the suffering for it.

But now after having done these things, what is the answer, what is the solution? The solution is to bring, to say again, mind to a quiet, the mind to a quiet state and then in that analysis repentance is involved and say, "May I have the strength not to do it again". So at this prison talk I gave which was televised, I said, I gave them hope. "You are all children of the Divine. Some little thing happened that put you here behind bars. But now look at it from the other side when you were outside, you had so many million worries, you had this to do and that to do and that to do. But now you are inside. What can you do? Meditate." So we started teaching them meditation and spiritual practices. "Meditate and bring yourself together so when you leave these iron gates, you'd be a better person and not repeat the things that you have done. But have hope. Have courage that you are the children of God. And here you have plenty of time to sit and think and analyze". Why don't all of you go to prison, the prison of your little room, the iron bars, because then society will ostracize you. How many time don't we find a person with a criminal record not being able to get jobs? You find that. So you see how society treats? It!s a cruel, cruel world. But I'm not going to be cruel. Say that to yourself, I am not going to be cruel to myself by punishing myself by remembering over and over again the past, instead of analyzing it. Because people say, "Oh, forget the past." Forget, you forget it, that could never happen. You could never forget the past. It will always come up in the mind and the only time when it cannot come up in the mind, is when you resolve the problem within yourself through repentance and say through repentance, a sincere feeling within. So I've killed a man, why can't I go around and try and save some people's lives. Become a life saver or some other work you can do, where you can make people happy, if you have made someone unhappy before. You see? So repentance, which is a kind of self-analysis, can also be put into action and the repentance has the greatest value if it is put into action.

'So I have made my mother unhappy', you would say. Are all the women in the world not your mothers? Make someone else happy for example, if your mother is not there anymore to make amends with. There are so many old age homes, so many poor old women living alone. So lonely. Because of your actions you have made someone blind. Go to some blind people, a Blind Institution for example, speak to them, give them comfort. They can't see, they can't read. Spend an hour or two reading for them, some book that they might want to, that are perhaps interested in and you'll bring joy and happiness to other's lives. Bring joy into the lives of other people and that is one means whereby, where we can get rid of our own karma and that is how we lead ourselves from darkness to light. *Om asato ma sad gamaya.* Lead me from untruth to truth. *Tamso ma jyotir gamaya.* Lead me from darkness to light. *Mrityor ma'amritam gamaya.* Lead me from death from mortality to immortality. It!s a beautiful Sanskrit prayer.

"You cannot destroy relativity and you cannot destroy the Absolute. But transcending the law of opposites, you become the observer of the law of opposites. Then good and bad disappears. It means you have risen above them. And when you rise above the law of opposites, nothing can affect you. For if you feel pleasure today, you can be sure the day after tomorrow you will feel pain. Pain and pleasure, good and bad are two sides of the same coin. They are made of the same energy and they co-exist as light and darkness co-exists. So the secret is to go beyond, to rise above and the only way to rise above, is to rise above the conscious level of the mind and through spiritual practices you reach the superconscious level and then you are at a vantage point whereby you can observe all these happenings. And the sun is hidden on the other half of the world and then this half seems dark. But does that mean light has disappeared and darkness has come or darkness has disappeared and light has come? No. This is the way the universe functions as it will always function and as it has functioned since eternity.

So in order to get away from our sufferings and miseries, we rise above it. So, in the same way the past must remain the past. The past is gone, the future might not come, the present is here and when you stand in the middle of the seesaw that goes up and down, good and bad, past and future, and when you stand in the middle of the seesaw, the seesaw stands still, because no pressure is put on either side. You are standing in the centre and the seesaw stands still for you although either end still exists."

If you stand in the centre of light and darkness, past and future, you have to stand in the center, within yourself, which is the Kingdom of Heaven within. One reaches the centre and that is the aim and goal of life. If I can't see the goodness in any man, there's nothing wrong with the man. What is wrong, is with me. I am the stumbling block. I am the block that prevents me from seeing the truth or prevents me from seeing the goodness in man. If I see anything bad in anyone then be sure to know that it is my own limitation and my own mental projection which I am projecting on the other person. Because who can judge who? You're only judging a person by his outward appearances or his outward actions. What do you know of his spiritual self? What do you know of his real self how good he is? A thief, smash and grab thief, he broke into a window and as he was running away he heard the police whistles. But as he was running away, he found a small child on the road and a car was coming fast. He stopped while running away picked up the child and brought it to the sidewalk and took the child to safety and still started running away. Of course he was caught and he paid his just dues for what he did. So which is the greater good of the two? Stealing the few tins of canned peas or beans in the shop or saving the child. Isn't he good? Ain't he good! Yeh.

Prison Satsang (US82031, Lorton, VA)

Gururaj explaining Pranayama: Breathing is brought into a rhythm. It regenerates your entire system. After you have a stressful day, for example, you will find that doing this about three times a day, half a dozen times each time, you'll find some great relaxation pouring into you. And when your body becomes more relaxed and calmer, you'll feel less of strain and less of stress. Not only that, with this calmness that is brought into the mood, you perform all your activities in a more coherent manner.

Now, if you could stand outside the universe you will find that the universe would be pulsating. And it would be pulsating at the same rate: four, sixteen, eight. So what you are actually doing by doing this very simple practice, while it is not meditation really, by doing this very simple practice, you are tuning yourself to the universe. By this very simple practice you draw upon yourself those universal energies which we could call Divine energies. Inhale to the count of four. Retain the breath to the count of sixteen and exhale to the count of eight. 4:16:8

Now, why greater control is required in exhalation is this, that by exhalation you are expelling toxins in our body. And when exhalation becomes complete, inhalation becomes easy. So all bodies have certain kinds of toxins in them, and this is one way how to get rid of toxins.

Questioner: I want to know where and who and when meditation came into existence or how it has first come about?

Gururaj: Meditation started existing thousands of years ago when man assumed his human form. Man has always been required to meditate. He might have been doing it unconsciously, but now there are methods whereby he can do it very consciously.

What happens in the process is this, that from the conscious level of the mind you enter the deeper levels of the subconscious mind, and then to that calm area, which I call the superconscious mind. And when through a systematic individualized process one enters the area of the superconscious mind, you draw from it the various energies that are there - Divine energies - and you allow these energies to permeate your subconscious mind, your mind and your body. By doing this stress is released. You become tranquil. You become more gentle. You feel an inner peace, the Kingdom of Heaven within. You find that peace permeating your daily actions.

So the more people start meditating will there be less conflict in the world. And conflict is caused by the three levels of the mind not functioning in an integrated manner. In other words the ordinary man functions very fragmentedly. And it is this fragmentation that causes the conflict of life. And if we can strengthen ourselves through these meditational and spiritual practices, we would be in a much better position to accept what life has given us.

Life has always given us joy. Inherently the inner force within you is joy, but because of the fragmentation of man's mind he does not experience joy. And when he does not experience joy, then he

170

tries to find some kind of joy. And that kind of joy, instead of finding it within himself, he tries to find it externally through various kinds of deeds. They could be good deeds or bad deed or whatever. That is not important. But his entire being is focused outwardly instead of inwardly where the real peace lies.

Now, my dear brothers, as I said before when I greeted you, that you are children of God. You are Divinity incarnate. That Divine force is within you all the time. If we believe Divinity to be omnipresent, being present everywhere, then that Divinity is present in every cell of your body. So you are living gods. Never mind what society says. Never mind what they say, because whatever society says is a projection of their own minds and not you. For who can really judge you? Judge ye not that ye be judged. No man is capable of judging another man. But we that may have been victims of circumstances. Many things that society has inflicted upon us. And many times it is a very unjust inflicting.

But now if we are placed in certain circumstance, what do we do? We try and accept the circumstance and make the best of it. Now, how do we make the best of it is by becoming integrated people. I wish I could live here. It'll be a good chance for me to practice deeper and deeper meditations. What a great opportunity in disguise. For everything, every adversity, contains some opportunity. And it is for us to realize that opportunity. There's a very favorite saying of mine: "Two men behind prison bars. One saw mud, the other saw stars." So wherever we are we have the capacity, we have the ability to see the glory, to see the stars instead of seeing the mud. So two men in the same circumstances, none different, in the same cell — and for all life itself is a prison.

A prison does not require four walls. Life itself is a prison to 99.9999% of human beings. They have imprisoned themselves within various conflicts that are in them.

But to remember this, that you are Divine. You are sinless. For the real Divinity within you is beyond all sin. It is beyond all suffering. You are purity itself. It is only the experiences that you have had that has created these veils, this opaqueness. So that the clarity of yourself is not seen, and with spiritual practices you slowly remove these veils so that you could face yourself squarely in the mirror and say, "Truly, I am divine." Then what will happen to you is this: All your fears will vanish. All your feelings of insecurity will vanish. All your feelings of inadequacy will vanish. All your guilts will vanish. All your jealousies will vanish. Covetousness will vanish. All these things that bring on greater and greater conflicts will vanish. And then you will say, "I am divine. You are divine. The universe is divine." You will lose that sense of me and mine, for all is thine and I am thee. So the free will gets transmuted into divine will and you live with divine will in divinity. That's the living God. That's the difference between the personal god and the impersonal God. The personal god is the totality of this universe. The impersonal God is the energy which energizes or gives momentum to the personal god that functions. So God, the personal god, is a mixture of everything, and everything is good. The sun shines hot and draws water vapor, which forms into clouds, hmm? And down here it is dark and dismal. And we say it is dark and dismal. And then the clouds must disperse in rain and we see the sun again. In the first place who made those dark clouds. The sun's heat--the sun? So is the sun a part and parcel of the water and the dark cloud? Do you see? So this entirety is but a process. It will--the sun, the light will evaporate the water into water vapor and it will become dark? And it's the same force when all the water vapor becomes so heavily laden that it will bring the rain, which in turn will grow the food you eat, huh? Make these flowers beautiful, huh? It would not be beautiful if we did not have those dark clouds. There would be no rain. Do you see. So everything is so beautiful and systematic. Only thing we think of the dark clouds. That's all we think. "Oh, what a dull day today." So miserable. But rise above that. It might be so miserable from down here, but go up in the airplane, the sun is untouched. Your inner self is untouched by any cloud that surrounds you.

Gururaj: They asked me to come and give a talk to the prisoners that were there in this prison. Long-term prisoners. I told them... You have made a mistake. OK. How many have not made mistakes? You were just unfortunate that you were caught. So forget that. And be thankful to divinity that you are in this prison. It will give you a greater chance to dive deep within yourself and make yourself a better person.

A fellow came to see me at my center in Cape Town, South Africa. And, he had been in jail for five years. So, he tried to get a job. But wherever--he had to tell the truth, because sooner or later the boss would find out. So he had to say, "I'm an ex-convict." And he couldn't get a job. And yet when I spoke to the man and meditated on him, I found him such a highly spiritually developed person. He had used his time in jail to really dive within himself. He came out a clean person. Being in jail was a wonderful bath to him, cleansing him. But nobody would give him a job. I had connections. I phoned a few firms that I knew and fixed him up with a good position. And he still is there for several years now and getting promotions every year. So you see. There is an adversity. There is an opportunity in every adversity. It's just how we use it, and what emphasis we put on things that's important.

Q: I hate to start the question again. But, what is the purpose of all this--our existence-to begin with? Has man reflected on that? Why did God create all this... for us to go through if we are God?

Gururaj. : Beautiful! The entire universe has no purpose whatsoever. It is eternal, immortal, was, is, and will be. And that which was, is, and will be has no purpose because God has no purpose. He just is. So, therefore, I said we do not live in a creation of God, but we live as a manifestation of God. And the things that you go through is nothing wrong at all. If you could only realize that everything that happens is a divine happening. If the mind could be unpatterned from sorrow and misery, then you will find that sorrow and misery does not exist. It all lies in your mind. If you walk through a dark street, and if you are afraid of muggers, every little stump or every little post box might seem like a mugger lurking around to attack you. Your mind. Meanwhile, while there are no muggers. But you have a purpose. And your purpose of life is to merge that individuality of yours into that universality. That is the end and aim and goal of you as an individual being. But when you come to this realization of the inner self through proper forms of meditation, you will discover that I--all the time--have had no individual being.

As human beings, we are always thinking. You expend more energy with negative and hateful thoughts than with uplifting thoughts. The scattered unruly mind jumps from one thought to another. Tranquility and silence can be found within once you know how to access it. Thoughts of love, kindness and compassion will not only help the receiver but it can also help the sender. In our lives, the purpose of meditation is to unpattern the patternings that keep coming up in the crevices of our minds. We have created our own inner demons with our own negative thinking. Harboring anger and self righteousness is not conducive to one's spirit. Thoughts, feelings and emotions can change the world. So it is expending eleven times more energy by thinking about it ten times. Why not just get onto it and it is done. And then sit down with a free mind and meditate if you have nothing else to do. You have come from nowhere and you are going nowhere. You are here. Here now. Now here! When this body is dropped, your soul the observer the observer (inner body), your subtle body (mind), goes to another plane of existence for evaluation; Time and space does not exist in the afterlife.

***

CHAPTER 18

AWAKENING TO WHO YOU REALLY ARE

As humans began to awaken, one of the oldest questions we ponder is "Who am I"? Philosophers have never been able to answer that question with certainty because that answer can only come from within yourself. It is not until the mind, body, and spirit become integrated that the answer dawns upon you and you emphatically say, "I am Divine!" Integration is required, not fragmentation. We have very fragmented minds, which cause all sorts of problems and anxieties as old repetitive thoughts play over and over like broken records. The conscious mind gets stuck in worm holes of thoughts circling again and again. Meditation helps us to rise above and out of those ruts as we become more integrated. When we go deeper into the subconscious mind our thoughts become more refined as we resonate with higher frequencies. Our intellects are awakened when our minds gain some understanding; then our hearts feel more love and compassion. It is as if the entire Universe opens up to us and we experience a sense of freedom. That is how meditation is an amazing way to find an inner life and ultimate freedom while serving time in prison. When we reach the superconscious level then we realize who we really are. We unfold to inner knowingness that is connected to all that is. Nothing can take away our spirits and our deep connection with Divinity. We are truly blessed. Grace surrounds us as we infuse spiritual energies in our everyday lives. Meditation benefits us by the serenity we feel while in the meditative states and continues because it makes us aware of impulsivity and reactivity.

Awaken to Your New Reality

Awaken to who we really are, which is Divinity itself, while living in our human bodies. Judgments from societal members and authority figures have fostered certain beliefs and standards for the elite seemingly having preferential treatment. When we emanate positivity and light we will notice that racial disparities decrease. Incarcerated individuals who are deemed unworthy suffer greater consequences than people on the outside.

After their release, it may be a little more difficult to get jobs to support themselves and their families; difficult, but certainly possible. All humans deserve to live in peace. It is crucial to have mutual respect, and for inmates to redeem themselves through job and social programs. Emotions of fear and anger often precipitate crimes. We are part of the Universe and humanity. Regardless of our faults and frailties that keep us locked up in our own minds, we can still experience a sense of freedom and inner peace. Changing our perspective can be a very effective way for relief from suffering. We often need to step back from the chaotic world in order to see the silver lining that resides behind every dark cloud or negative situation. Learning to make the best of a bad situation and accept our current state or condition while infusing light to allow proper understanding is essential. With meditation and spiritual practices, we heal from the inside out. We all have certain life lessons that teach us how we contribute to the wellbeing of humanity. We all have a role to play. If we make mistakes we must learn how to let them go. It does no good whatsoever to continue to harbor resentment or shame. When we have insight into the subtle forces of the world around us and learn how to take responsibility for our thoughts and actions, we search for truth about ourselves and accept what really happened. Stop saying "I'm a sinner" or "I'm no good." Look for your own goodness and focus on the things you have done right instead of ruminating about what you did wrong! Perhaps your misdeeds can catapult you into a new way of life. Or you can teach others based on your own experiences. When you have conquered your own inner demons and fears that have been part of your life experience, you will find ways to support the lives of others. The world is not going to end because of something you did or said or due to your actions or inactions. Maybe we need to learn how to lessen the ego's need to be right? Labeling yourself as a drug addict, gang member, or bad person keeps you stuck in never ending cycles of blame and shame. The key is how do we unlock our minds that keep us stuck in vicious cycles of right and wrong? Reliving our stories is not the way to heal. How do we unlock our minds to experience freedom on the inside?

When you look at your life and say, "There are no mistakes" you will see why you had to learn certain lessons by being incarcerated. Uncovering your essence and finding your place in the world by changing your perspective to see the good that is inherent in bad situations regardless of where you are, can awaken you to your inner self and connection to the Divine. Regardless of where we are, in prison, a war zone, or on the streets, we can acclimate and find the blessing. Having gratitude for being alive is sometimes all we need to change ourselves and the conditions we find ourselves in. Acknowledging the things in your life that you could have done differently and seeking a happier more peaceful life may be just what we need to lift you up out of the drudgeries of life. Never underestimate your value and power to change yourself and the world around you. When you align yourself with the Universe and Divinity with sincerity and purpose, miracles can happen. Prayer and meditation are tools that can lift us up and clear our eyes from veils of grief and sorrow. You will see how important you are and can provide service to your brother man in prison and to humanity on the outside. So many people are asleep and like the walking dead. They do not realize the power that lies within. When they began to realize that they have created their own reality by attracting negative energy as a result of their own negative emanations, then they have learned how to manifest and align themselves with people and situations in their lives for their betterment. Living in the now helps to create a better future. Self empowerment can uplift us and humanity to new heights. When self aggrandizement ceases, it is easier to become one with Divinity. Living in the present moment can acclimate us to the difficult prison environment. There is so much suffering that occurs when people are not seeing reality. It is as if people are living in their own dreams or nightmares. Meditation practices can awaken sleeping spirits and bring new fresh energy into our lives. What life lessons need to be experienced to teach us about ourselves?

The power of meditation cannot be underestimated. Learning how to manage fear and anger and paying attention to the emotional triggers that arise from time to time will teach us certain lessons. With regularity in practice, meditation can shine a light on the dark recesses of our minds that regurgitate old worn out memories and information. If we constantly re-live these negative memories we keep ourselves stuck within the confines of our own minds. Poor self esteem and role models do not allow space, and a sense of freedom from thinking about past mistakes. When we have awareness and understand how we got here, only then can we do something to get ourselves out of the chains that keep us from moving forward with our lives. Ancient teachings offer insight and new ways for hope and healing. I want to provide other light workers like teachers and healers with information about the mind, body, and spirit, and how awareness plays a role in manifesting good positive energy. Their service is very much needed in the prison environment. They too can contribute to the wellbeing of humanity, by offering their skills to the underserved prison population who are dealing with despair, perhaps as a result of bad choices. Everyone makes mistakes and deserves a chance for redemption. Instead of using punishment as the only form of redemption we must use other methods to uplift them, so they can pay it forward and contribute to humanity. Not everyone has gotten a fair shake.

Spending years of their lives incarcerated, inmates have time and space without the distractions of living in the outer world. Many of them have never been exposed to segments of society where there are resources. It is possible to synthesize whatever religious ideology they have once their awareness increases. It is a blessing to have the awareness to see the One Source of all of humanity and the essence of religions, so they are integrated rather than separated and fragmented. Unfortunately, many people are fear oriented instead of loving each other's differences. Instead, we tend to judge others who are different from us. Everyone, regardless of the misdeeds they have performed has the possibility of redemption. I often wonder what life experiences and circumstances contributed to this present moment of incarceration?

CHAPTER 19
RESOURCES

Offering positive resources such as prison ministry, meditation and mindfulness programs can free prisoners from being locked up in the body and mind, thereby giving them a new lease on life. Resources that promote positive understanding and learning opportunities have life changing effects on inmates but they also create better functioning prison systems that encourage peace over hostility and violence.

Many prisons offer offenders educational resources and opportunities. Some of these programs include Alcoholics Anonymous and Narcotics Anonymous. There are also religious services and support groups for Christians, Muslims, Buddhists, etc. They are all supported by volunteers. The inmates share dialogue, meditation, and prayer with like-minded spirits. Some inmates feel powerless, and hopelessness prevails, pulling them into negative spirals of depression and despair. These programs are an important part of the healing process as the inmates come to terms with their faults and frailties. There are tremendous lifelong benefits to having the opportunity to improve their lives by learning new skills and ways of coping with the challenges and personal struggles of living in the prison environment and beyond.

The penal system does not cure the ills of society but it serves a purpose by keeping incarcerated individuals from perpetuating further crimes. Unfortunately, racial disparities exist. Black and brown skinned people are overrepresented disproportionately in jail populations. In 2020, they were imprisoned five times more than the rate for white individuals. Depending on the prison and state and federal laws, prison can be a source of punishment. However, some can also be a source of healing. Even though helpful programs exist, nothing can replace freedom.

There will always be unawakened beings who do not take responsibility for their actions. They blame their parents, their victims, society, and when they can't blame anyone else, they blame God. They find themselves trapped in situations and seem powerless to control their emotions, which get expressed by their egoic minds. Some inmates are set in their ways and insist that others are to blame for their demise. Once the chains that have physically locked them up have been removed, they still are locked up in their minds and have difficulty freeing themselves. Freedom is found within! It is only when they reflect back on their mistakes and take responsibility for their own actions that they can make progress and move forward. It is true that the ills of society have to bear some responsibility, especially when innocent people have been locked up. Unfortunately, some people in lower socioeconomic brackets serve more time than people in higher economic brackets, which seems unfair. Some criminals are actually victims who have been serving time for being at the wrong place at the wrong time. They have not been exonerated and are trapped in unfair criminal justice systems waiting for someone to set them free. Families and some segments of society are negatively affected, keeping them stuck in never ending cycles of punishment and shame. Workforce development programs that offer incarcerated individuals educational programs to learn new trades or skills are beneficial and offer a new lease on life and a sense of hope and exoneration. It is easier to reintegrate in society when job opportunities are available, which reduces the chances of becoming repeat offenders.

Doreena Durbin

According to Federal Bureau of Prisons (BOP), Inmate Offenses, 44.4% of people are serving time in prison as a result of drug offenses, which include selling, buying, or using. Most mental disorders in the prison population are severe depression followed by generalized anxiety disorder.[10]

According to a study from Reuters: Health News, Oct. 12, 2016, regularity in practicing of meditation was linked to lower stress levels among prison inmates.[11] A reduction of psychological shocks, severe distress symptoms, and sleep problems was shown to be beneficial for physical and mental health. This study found that rates of recidivism drop. A meditation program for inmates promotes peace and supports the work and dedication of the prison ministry program. Prisoners who are isolated from the outside world learn ways to fill up their down times with positive practices.

Women's Prisons

My deepest apologizes go to my sisters in prison who would also benefit from having a meditation program. I am hoping other teachers can provide meditation programs in women's prisons as well. However, everything in this book applies to women as well as men. My focus has been on men's prisons because I have actual experience teaching in them. Growing up with three brothers helped to toughen me up and prepare for this service. There are fewer women serving time and there are typically much lower security levels in women's prisons. In a 2007 National Crime Victimization Study, according to the Department of Justice 75.6% of offenders are men, which includes violent crimes, while 20.1% are women.[12] Women tend to violate drug or property laws and have a history of spousal or family abuse leading to mental health disorders such as depression, anxiety, and PTSD. Also, sexual abuse creates many other conflicts in the mind, including self esteem issues.

OTHER RESOURCES
Books

A great self help book that I had read decades ago was introduced during one of my classes at the suggestion of one of the inmates. I brought two copies for the guys to read then pass on to others. I felt it was very relevant to their progress. Learning how to incorporate new skills, with simple, easy to remember teachings will help them on their life paths.

The Four Agreements: A Toltec Wisdom Book by Don Miguel Ruiz is a teaching tool to shine a light on the source of self limiting beliefs.[13]

The Four Agreements are:

1. Be Impeccable with Your Word,
2. Don't Take Anything Personally,
3. Don't Make Assumptions, and
4. Always Do Your Best.

CHAPTER 20

LOOKING TOWARDS THE FUTURE

Stay Out of Prison! Trust your gut.

God's grace is equal for all beings regardless of judgment by court systems or society. Many people in our society have committed crimes and did not have to serve time in prison. They just didn't get caught! Everyone is equal but we are conditioned by society, our churches, our parents, and our teachers. Since the time we were born, we have been told, "Don't do this" or "Don't do that." Certain norms are ok in some cultures but they are wrong in other cultures and countries. There are some cultures that believe in polygamy while others would consider it immoral. Moral laws have been created by man, not God. Purity is more important then morality in God's laws. Feeling guilty and miserable is not the way to learn and face the truth. You must admit your indiscretions by accepting what you have done. I accept that I have done this or made a mistake. Ask yourself why you did whatever you have done wrong, then meditate or pray sincerely asking for the Lord's forgiveness. Remember what Christ said on the cross, "Father, forgive them, they know not what they do." You can ask God for forgiveness for yourself too. At the time of your indiscretion you might have not been aware when certain acts were done, especially in drug or alcohol induced states of unawareness. When you harm someone, you actually harm yourself more.

Mental torture will stay in your mind causing you more suffering. When you learn how to quiet the mind, then you can ask for repentance and strength that you will never repeat the negative act that keeps you stuck in never-ending cycles. There is always hope.

Intuition is a natural gift that is given to all humans. Some are more developed than others but as part of the animal kingdom we all have the gift of intuition. It is one of our defense mechanisms. Our bodies are superb instruments to warn us of danger. It is with us all of the time if we just pay attention to our senses. Our five senses including sight, sound, touch, taste, and smell are designed to keep us safe. Our solar plexus or manipura (third chakra, located near the navel) has radiating nerve fibers which are located in the abdomen. It is for helping you feel in control of your life. Your gut is part of the intestinal system near the stomach. When we have bad feelings they are often indicators that we need to pay attention to our thoughts and actions. Our instinct helps keep us safe. When you are advised to trust your gut, it is our intuitive faculties that we must pay attention to when making decisions. How many times have we all made bad decisions even though our instinct or gut was telling us otherwise? One of the methods I have used is to put my attention on my gut when I have to make a difficult decision. If you are in the company of so called friends who tell you to go in with a gun and rob a store and your gut and mind are going through somersaults and machinations, stop before you act! Your intuition will get your attention. Look beyond to the consequences of your actions. It is in those times of knowing that it is most important to pay attention to your gut. This can apply to all sorts of things in life like avoiding accidents, relationships, buying a house or car, or deciding which job to accept. If you put your attention on your gut and get a nervous uncomfortable feeling, then you know it is the wrong decision. On the other hand, if after putting your attention on your gut, and you get a good comfortable feeling, then you know that is the right decision.

If your Guardian Angel, or Jesus could talk with you now, what might they say? "You did nothing wrong. You are loved and cherished forever. You will be taken care of. You have nothing to fear."

"What is happening to our young people? They disrespect their elders, they disobey their parents. They ignore the law. They riot in the streets, inflamed with wild notions. Their morals are decaying. What is to become of them?" Plato, 428-347 BC

Funny the way some things repeat themselves. Was Plato seeing into the future?

Tips for Wellbeing:

- It is not the situation itself, but it's about how you react to it that causes stress.

- Look at the big picture. Ask yourself, "Is this really that bad? Is this a life or death situation or something that I should be able to get over quickly?"

- Align yourself with Universal energy by doing the deep breathing, which stimulates the parasympathetic nervous system and helps rest, restore, and expand the lower lungs. The 4:16:8 breathing practice is a quick and easy way to calm down and to come back to alignment.

- Pay attention to negative thinking.

- Analyze your emotions. Be aware of any anger and frustration that arises as it travels through your body. Breathe into the tension rather than contracting and over-reacting.

- Embrace adversity.

- Avoid despair. Flight feelings of hopelessness and defeat. Stress increases adrenaline. Use it to your advantage by actively dealing with one problem at a time.

- Always do your best. Rise to the challenge, give it your all, and then let it go. There is no use dwelling on the past.

CHAPTER 21

SCIENCE

Experience the Quantum Field of All Possibilities While Serving Time.

Before I begin this section, I just want to say that for some of you, this section on quantum physics might make your eyes glaze over. Believe me, mine did too when I first embarked upon this particular topic several decades ago. I firmly believe that my meditation practice was the largest contributor to opening up my mind, as my neural network continued to make connections with other neurons. Never having the opportunity to take high school physics, due to prerequisite changes in the three different high schools I attended in Florida and Illinois, I was restricted from taking science classes, but that did not restrict me. It just pushed me forward to continue learning in spite of the restrictions. I believe that a combination of curiosity, intuition, and meditation attributed to my deeper understanding of not only science but also languages. As one language opened up to me I began to understand the connectedness of other languages as well. Perhaps it was just plain stubbornness and not wanting to appear stupid, while working for many years with surgeons and doctors, that challenged me to want to expand my knowledge and understanding of the world around me. I was always fascinated by science and the cosmos. Richard Feynman, an American theoretical physicist who collaborated in the nuclear program used to say... "Don't be upset if you do not understand quantum, nobody understands it." *Domain of Science*, Feb. 25, 2019.

Quantum physics is the study of the properties and behaviors of particles at a subatomic level. We are quantum particles not limited in space and time. Our beliefs stand between us and experiencing the great potential the Universe has for us. In the quantum field of all possibilities as an observer we co-create with Divinity to manifest our highest dreams. We are free to create because our minds are free. We feel empowered to be part of, rather than separate from, quantum experiences. Science has taught us that energy cannot be created or destroyed. Everything is energy; even our minds and thoughts carry an energetic imprint. The chair we are sitting on is made of microscopic particles. Each particle is energy. We do not need a phone or social media to send love and prayers to others. Others will receive forgiveness on an energetic level when we send love. Others do not need to be aware of what we are doing. Real healing comes from a pure source, not from the ego.

The Universe is teeming with powerful energies and we are co-creators in the quantum field of all possibilities. Do we really see what we think we see? Is it real or is it unreal? In Hinduism, another term for illusion is *maya*. There is a connection between meditation and quantum mechanics. Consciousness is experienced during meditative states; however, everything in nature has consciousness. The observer effect in consciousness during meditation and quantum mechanics are similar. In the quantum theory the nature of matter as well as the behavior of subatomic particles behave in an odd way, where quantum particles can have both particles and waves simultaneously. Subatomic particles can be in several places, which is why the quantum theory is so difficult to measure and understand. Everything around you is made of subatomic particles. What is real and what is unreal depends on the observer. Some researchers theorize that objectivity is an illusion. They discovered that if

189

we observe an object, it exists. Just like the question about a tree falling in a forest...with no one around to hear it. Does it really make a sound? An object in nature changes its behavior depending upon our observation of it. Our reality is a reflection of our thoughts, attitudes, beliefs, and emotional states.

Albert Einstein was known for his theory of relativity ($E=mc^2$) and had a difficult time reconciling classical physics with quantum physics. Einstein once wrote that he can't believe that God would choose to play dice with the Universe. He thought that there should be actual outcomes instead of just mere chances. There is a theory that suggests that quantum objects can be in two places simultaneously; the exact location of a particle in space cannot be predicted. Oppenheimer studied quantum mechanics as it was rising in popularity as a new way of thinking.

Technology continues to evolve. Artificial Intelligence (AI) is exponentially spreading globally and causing fear and mistrust. Humanity is being affected by new technology and science. Outdated ways of thinking will keep us stuck in the past as the world continues to evolve. In 1825 when the first trains exceeded 30 miles per hour, people were mortified fearing that their bodies could not withstand those speeds. Radios were distracting children just like media devices are doing today. With free will, we can go down kicking and screaming or we can rise up and find the good in the progress we make as we continue to evolve. We live in a big world, which appears to be getting smaller and smaller as new technology increases and old technology is becoming obsolete.

CHAPTER 22

GOING FORWARD IN FREEDOM

"For to be free is not merely to cast off one's chains, but to live in a way that respects and enhances the freedom of others." Nelson Mandela

I convey to the inmates that they are powerful beyond measure—not from an egotistical or physical standpoint but because they are connected to Source. Our souls are free and cannot be contained. Learn everything you can while you are incarcerated. Take advantage of uplifting or educational programs. Do not waste your life. You are too valuable to waste your time pursuing things that do not serve your highest good. The world needs you with all of your strengths. Don't ever think you are not good enough or smart enough. Everyone has unique talents. They just need to be uncovered. There is always something you can do. Never, never feel like a failure. You are worthy and Divine.

Whatever happens to us is really for our own benefit. Perhaps we need challenges in our lives to wake us up. When we don't have challenges, we become complacent. As challenges arise it is important to see the gift that is inherent within them. Meditation is a Divine gift. Go forward in love and freedom and create the life you desire. You have been given tools; you just need to use them. Life is pouring through you here and now. That energy is palpable.

Doreena Durbin

"Arise! Awake! Stop Not Until the Goal is Reached." Swami
Vivekananda

Be a Source of Positive Change

Whenever you feel anger towards others, surround them with
white light. It will not only help your enemy but it will also help you
to release negative emotion that you have allowed to disempower
you. In reality, if you hurt others, you hurt yourself.

*Albert Einstein used to say that weak people seek revenge, strong
people forgive and intelligent people ignore.*

We are participating in making the world better. Do your part. Be
a source of change. Be true to yourself and others. Be your best
self. Do not do to others what you do not want done to yourself.
In other words, treat others the way you want to be treated. Honor
yourself and everyone around you. When do you fight and when
do you accept? You must discriminate between causes worth
standing up and fighting for. Is the fight really worth it? What was
the motivation? If it was to bolster the ego then that would be a
mistake. Determine if you are fighting for the greater good or just
to satisfy your own ego. If you decide it was a worthy cause, then
acceptance is the next step, whatever the outcome. The Serenity
Prayer, which was written by an unknown author around 1936-
1942 is useful when needing to accept what is: "God grant me the
serenity to accept the things I cannot change, courage to change
the things I can, and wisdom to know the difference." The Serenity
Prayer is helpful for people in recovery from addictions to alcohol
and/or drugs. Never let the sadness of your past and the fear of
the future ruin the happiness of your present. Sometimes things
have to go very wrong before they can go right. Overthinking will
destroy your inner peace. Let it go. Breathe! You didn't go through
all of this for nothing.

CHAPTER 23
GRATITUDE

I am deeply grateful for having the opportunity to teach at this prison, which has provided me with a sense of hope for a fairer and more just system for incarcerated individuals, especially with programs like meditation. These men are amazing. Their spirits are strong as they navigate life in the best way they know. Meditation is an invaluable lifelong gift. Serving time does not have to be devoid of hope. This book will hopefully inspire others to incorporate meditation into their lives. Many people fear the unknown and are reluctant to go into prisons. I am hoping to remove the barriers and fears so that other teachers and healers who want to provide their services to this disadvantaged population can help make our societies safer and more conducive to wellbeing. Uplifting the inmates and awakening their hearts is crucial for emotional healing, not only for the inmates but also for their families. Not only are the incarcerated individuals physically separated in the confines of prison but they are also serving time within their minds as they ruminate about what they could have done differently to stay out of jail. After the offense(s) some inmates feel powerless and a sense of hopelessness prevails. Valuable lessons of love and forgiveness for themselves and others can be found during reflection, contemplation, and meditation. These lost or forgotten souls still have a purpose in life. There may be times in our own lives where we could have committed crimes of passion, while drinking or using drugs. Many of us could have been jailed but we

Doreena Durbin

escaped or just didn't get caught. All people deserve a chance for redemption. Freedom is found within.

As inmates continue on their life journeys, I hope this book serves to remind them of the things we talked about and learned in our classes. I encourage them to pay it forward by serving their fellow man in prison. All beings are connected to the One Source. I want them to know that they are powerful beyond measure and that their prison experience should not define them. I also want them to know that they are worthy and loved, regardless of their misdeeds. God has not given up on them so why should we? Once incarcerated individuals learn new ways of thinking, embracing new concepts, they will realize that they still have value. They can teach others to follow a better path leading to a more spiritual life. Real healing takes place when meditation and prayer are incorporated into daily life.

Chapter 24

PERSONAL EXPERIENCES FROM INMATES

To respect the privacy of the inmates I am only using their first initials. The inmate writings are written in their own words. None of their writings have been edited with the exception of minimal punctuation for clarity.

D: Get a Life.

These were the first thoughts I recall screaming into my head as the heavy metal door slammed shut confining me into the first holding cell in my initial trip to jail. So early on I realized I needed to change my ways of living life and change thinking. I bonded out of jail days later but arrest #2 three months later had me hearing the same metal doors slamming me in again. Realizing this stay would be longer the voice became a demanding shout to "Get a life before life destroys me!" Facing a 10-year sentence I had ample time to prepare my better life but 18 months in I was granted parole and never got past getting a prison life. A few years passed before arrest #3 and a third time listening to those familiar metal doors restrain me. I remember feeling absolute dread at the realization that my pattern of behaviors might result in an even longer sentence. That internal voice was now an angry, desperate scream that shocked my deepest attention. "I need to get a life" with the help of some force with great powers to overcome my stubborn ways and self-centered impediments. I knew then my mind had too much control over my logic that still sprouted up occasionally. I decided to seek God who I believed was out there somewhere, idly waiting for me to make contact so I could learn and accept the conditions of a sort of contractual arrangement we might negotiate. I recall having a level of awareness that a face, a spirit, could be called upon to bring relief to myself. That awareness was strongest when I was silent, when the world around me was still. Three years of incarceration, which followed allowed for some distraction-free dedication to this search, which did bare some sustainable fruit to nourish my soul. The most profound and productive opportunity came from a medical scare I unwillfully produced that triggered a medical isolation for three weeks in solitary confinement; 21 days of silence, aloneness, stillness. Outside movement consisted of watching clouds pass by in the small window near the ceiling or the mouse that visited when I was motionless or the sound of a food tray sliding under the door from a voiceless guard. The first few days were pure torment on my psyche. I had no escape no "tap out" option. I had no choice but to go inward, go deeper. When they unlocked the door on day 21, I didn't want to leave. Within a year I was forced out of the prison system and into another paroled release. It tested my resilience and a fourth experience at the metal door shutting sound came to be. This time my internal voice was softer, a bit worn out and my demand of myself a little simpler." I need to get a life that consider of nothing more than peace and joy." I need to get an inner life. It was at times, with a deep sense of surrender that a moment of enlightenment revealed that if I can abide in inner peace and navigate through the rest of life experiencing a resounding, sustained feeling of joy, what more would be necessary? That's what the process is all about. Finding that open door, not slamming it shut but walking through it, inward to achieve ongoing inner peace and sustained joy in everything that life provides us. What more is there to need?

This 15 year roadtrip I've described on my overall journey to becoming the true being, I AM is a testimony to roadblocks, potholes and mind traffic jams that are so easily and often faced on the trail of life. The ego is the part of our mind that creates a sense of 'self' identification. Every time we start a sentence with "I am" it's attempting to define who we are and how we want to be recognized by others. Ego is not about arrogance but about association. The human I am believes I am a felon, I am a 3-time convict, I am stubborn, I am entitled to... But this really is not who I am. For those who have a biblical aptitude, the phrase 'I AM That I AM' is powerful. It's significance is even deeper when you compare it with the ego's "I am". The most useful outcome of my commitment and diligence to a meditation practice is the discovery of my ultimate relationship with the I AM. "Be still and know I AM", Christian gnostic translation more precisely references that statement from God as: "Be still and know that I AM that I AM. In otherwords, still your mind (meditate) and experience your non-separation from all that exists. Come to know I AM the spirit that resides in your human being-ness and hang tight for a powerful ride through the rest of your life. Clearly, if a 4-time repeat offender who's stuck in stubbornness navigating life as a megalomaniac can figure out inner peace and joy, so can anyone. It doesn't take much beyond the will to get an inner life. The result is a peaceful contentment with all life throws at us. While I have not arrived at my destination of abiding in inner peace and joy, I'm getting closer. The pull of distraction weakens, the potholes of torment and sense of suffering still come up, but it's less frequent, short lived and easier to get back on smoother ground. The passage of time sharpens the mastery of my drive and that final destination feels within reach.

D: Week 2 of our Lockdown.

Unfortunately for me it means the end is just a few days away. I recognize that I am the odd man out in this feeling. Everyone else is 'stir crazy' and there is growing consensus that complete boredom is growing and becoming unbearable. I feel the complete opposite. I recognize what causes this since I now have the capacity of being positioned inward and thus able to observe what's outward. This advantage on life has come in part with a daily practice of meditation. What I'm observing is the preconditioned mind at work alongside the established habit of dependency that one has for other people and other things to keep us engaged, entertained and standing at attention. It's a common example of allowing life to be managed from the control of outside forces instead of the more powerful and controllable SELF or more deeply the divine self or 'true self'.

This understanding gets to the very cause of why the U.S. Criminal Justice System is failing to produce rehabilitated ex-felons at acceptable rates. The convicted are being 'blessed' and 'saved' by being removed from further destruction to self and others with the expectation by them and the system that houses them is that someone, something, some process (outside factor) will be what transforms and rehabilitates their inner being. This model results in nothing more than a mass incarceration of men/women who sit around fighting boredom, expecting to be entertained, enlightened, energized as they count down the days to release.

However, there is evidence that motivation and determination to improve oneself exists within the confines of guarded walls and razor wire. During lockdowns as with any typical daily routine the vast majority of inmates make time, find space and create tools to workout. Building the body into a bigger, muscular mass and a trim and tone physic commands discipline and action. In prison it's by far the most popular and visible activity that can be attributed to rehabbing. The results of the effort are noticeable. Those results can vary depending on how creative one gets at building heavier weights of resistance from common items found among inmate property. Cases of bottled water and dozens of books are accumulated not for drinking or reading, but for lifting. Bedding and towels are pulled and tied together to facilitate push-ups and pull-ups. Skinny inmates are solicited, put in place and balanced just right for added weight. These sessions occur daily and for hours by the faithful. In some circumstances to get the results one aspires to it involves breaking established housing rules or performing the routines discretely.

All this energy, effort and ingenuity to put forth every day in every prison across the country. All for the sake of becoming a better man. But becoming a better man of what: a more muscular and physically fit body which becomes more feared, more forceful, more sexually irresistible.

This is testimony to the untapped power and resourcefulness that currently exists in the captive incarcerated population and the immense potential that can be realized if the attention and intention is directed towards a workout that builds a more resistant, fit and trim inner-being that has ultimate commandment over that physical being.

D's letter during quarantine, 2/27/24

Doreena,

I have a heavy heart for missing today's experience led by you. I can't overly express how much I look forward to these days. This COVID quarantine will last about 5 days. Our faith-based functions have ceased during it so I have more time to focus on my writing, which will eventually transform into content to consider. Namaste.

J: The Book

I have always been in church. Since I was 5 years old I've been told to go to church and seek God. And make sure you live right and always put God first! Oh yea, always have faith! And talk to him through prayer! Prayer for wisdom and knowledge.

I have always walked and talked a certain way when it comes to God hoping it would take me places I have never been and wanted to go. And it did not … but I have always been told to keep faith! Let God lead you and talk to you! As I got deeper in the word because just a good word of motivation to keep living right or a certain way. And it became a way of life … But then it became depression half the time. And leaving me with holes in my life and think that I'm living wrong. So I started looking and seeing any kind of spiritual ways that God would speak to me, and lead me into some find of happiness, some kind of balance in my life! For years that's what I did until someone told me about meditation. And then it was explained to me how it works. How it can put balance in my life. And when you have your meditation session, it's the time where you let God speak to you! That way, it's supposed to be peaceful and your mind can stop for you to find peace but it don't. Well, it's hard to stop the mind. But it does allow you to think clearly about what it is that is troubling you. Resolving the grief, disrupts the truth and awakens to your purpose so you can love with purpose…Meditation.

R: A Newcomer's Initial Experience with Meditation.

My experience with meditation started when I saw a class on it was offered in our Chapel every other week. I was curious about it so I asked a friend of mine in my dorm who was going to the class what this "meditation thing" was all about. He gave me a good explanation of his experience but I was still leery due to my preconceived notions. I knew my friend also attended an "Eastern" religion class, so I assumed meditation had something to do with Buddhism or Hinduism. I was wrong about that.

What I found meditation to be wasn't what I thought. It wasn't in competition with my Christian based religion, which is what I feared. On the contrary, instead of competing with my religion, it actually complemented my Protestant background. And complemented it quite well. It wasn't some sort of self induced trance similar to hypnosis, another preconceived notion of mine.

What I found meditation to be was, in fact, an enhancement to my religion. It was actually part of my religion all along, although I didn't know it. There's a verse in the Bible, Psalm 46:10 that says, "Be still and know that I am God" and that's what meditation is to me. I had never given meditation a real try. Not to mention I didn't know how to do it. Then I started going to class and learned a little.

I learned about my breathing and counting breaths. I learned about how to sit and how to try to clear my mind by always coming back to my count on my breathing. The best I can describe my feeble attempts at meditation so far is that I became "hyper-focused" on the here and now. I'm not sure how apt a description that is but it's the best I can come up with. Another way I think it affects me is after I meditate I feel very "grounded" or stable. I don't know if that makes sense to anyone else but it does to me. Another word I can relate to is "centered". So far, I haven't committed to trying it as a daily ritual but I think I'm finally ready to give it a try on a daily basis. I'm expecting great results. I hope to write again and update my experience. If anyone is thinking about trying out meditation, I would wholeheartedly recommend it.

Signed,
Anonymous

D: The Influence of Distraction.

A benefit of being subjected to judicial imprisonment is the forced removal of life's countless distractions and their reverberating influence at keeping one down. They are powerful, irresistible and most times, overwhelming. We don't realize this until distractions are taken away and we can resist their return while in the culture of an incarcerated community. The detriment that distractions fuel is beyond notice until its influence diminishes. Anyone who

Doreena Durbin

has sat in a jail cell overnight or for an extended stay must have recognized, however briefly that distractions had been destroying focus, killing concentration and discouraging positive gain on life. During the initial realization of the perils from defeat when stillness becomes, the inner self awakens and reveals that distractions prohibited the sense of self-discovery, disconnected our intrinsic nature and impeded self actualization.

It was during my fourth trip back behind razor wire as I timed my EGO that I recognized the insurmountable stronghold that life's typical distractions had on holding me down from experiencing stillness within. It had blocked the portal that leads to the Ultimate Power of the Spirit Being I am. It obstructed my ability to guide my human beingness into a state of inner peace and resounding joy. Since the EGO is devoted to strengthening and preserving human self identity it uses the unwielding depth and breadth of distraction to control and curtail inward focus and replace it with self indulgent attention. The EGO prohibits the evolution of spirit, wisdom and well-being.

The elimination of distraction starts with focused awareness of my surroundings and their influence on my 5 senses, my human carnal desires, my monkey mind, my fears and prides, the default to live in the past or future. All are obstacles to consume, control, crack my inner drive to be set free; to abide in peace and be in constant joy. Being locked out of worldly ways is a blessed weapon provided to defeat the continual sway of distraction. I developed gratitude for this opportunity because without it I realized my battle to reach attention and intention of an inner life would be futile. As I kept distraction controlled awareness developed at the influences of every emotion, thought, action, every minute spent in my influenced reality was a delusion perception of reality completely filtered through the EGO, the controller of distraction and not through my true inner self-my Spirit Being. This delusion was unveiled through my dedicated efforts of asking myself one simple yet profound question at each distraction I encountered:

202

Is this (thought) (activity) (emotion) (time spent) getting me closer to the results (inner peace and joy) that I seek? For every 'No' answer I tossed it into the distraction trash can. It overflowed quickly and constantly at first. Over time the influence of distraction was overcome by the Power of Awareness. I manifested into the abidement of inner peace and joy. This mind exercise found strength and endurance only after I supplemented it with a routine of meditation. It's the muscle of the pursuit. A sustained meditation practice had to be taken as seriously as the devotion to Rec-time or a jailhouse weight lifting regiment. Exercising the inner self (soul) is no different from exercising the human body. Both take determination and dedication. Both manifest results. However, a trim, muscular physique eventually meets a law of impermanence and immortality and generates a satisfied ego. The Soul is eternal, infinite and omnipotent. A strong soul sets us free, not a strong body nor an unlocked prison gate.

R: Love your spirit more!

The aspiring writer in me wanted a bunch of adjectives added, a lot of big words so I could impress you with my exhaustive vocabulary. I was going to talk about heightened awareness and enlightened perception, augmented focus and altered states. Throw in talk of harmonic frequencies or vibrations that lead to a greater reality...

All that sounds so superficial. Meditation is just peaceful, it just calms me. It is somehow cleansing and refreshing. It basically soothes my soul. You know what I mean, huh? All those big words just confuse and cloud the issue.

As far as my sentence goes, I have 7 years left on my sentence. I'm here on my 3rd DWI but you never know about parole. God willing I could go home soon hopefully.

God bless, R

Doreena Durbin

R: There you are... Yay!

I was so glad to see your name pop up in my inbox. I knew you would have replied sooner if you could have. I suspected the problem was on my end but I'm just glad to be able to send and receive messages again.

Before I forget let me thank you for your efforts to find a replacement teacher so our classes can continue. It is just another example of the dedication and the commitment you have for empowering others on their spiritual journey through meditation. What I see in you inspires me to continue on my newfound path.

The results I'm obtaining from meditation are positive and impacting my life in many beneficial ways. This motivates me to keep pressing forward into... What? I'm not sure what? Divinity? Oneness? The Infinite?

I ain't sure where my newfound path leads but I'm digging it. Nothing but good vibes on this journey so far. I'm learning so much along the way. And I am so very grateful

to you. That you were there to help me as I embarked into the unknown... Just wanted you to know.

God bless, R.

R.: Words of Gratitude

I finally got my new tablet today. It's been almost 3 weeks since my old tablet crashed. I didn't know how much I would miss it until I didn't have it. Anyway, I now have a brand new tablet. Yay!

Thank you for your kind words. You're very thoughtful, kind and considerate. Character traits that are hardly ever displayed in institutions like this. And you give of a very good vibe and tons of positive energy too :).

You really are a breath of fresh air in here. You have no idea Doreena. I feel like I have been so lucky to have you this past year or so. You're an AWESOME teacher and you have taught me so much. I'm very grateful our paths have crossed. Meditation has helped me a great deal in a lot of different ways. I know I am a better man now that I've included meditation in my spiritual journey.

I've noticed the positive cumulative effect since I've started practicing a daily ritual of meditation at least once a day, although I often have two sessions a day. I hope you've noticed that I send you positive energy sometimes as I'm coming out of a meditation. I send it to different people as God puts them on my heart.

God bless, R.

CHAPTER 25
TEACHERS

I honor all of my teachers who have touched me deeply and helped me uncover inner wisdom. They have all taught me about life, including Jesus, the Buddha, and the Natives whose ancient teachings have been the bedrock of my journey. One of the most influential teachers of my lifetime is Gururaj Ananda Yogi (1932 - 1988) whom I met in 1977. He has been instrumental in changing the trajectory of my life and opening doors that I could never have imagined. Practicing and teaching meditation have enriched my life. He inspired me to teach others who are on the path of awakening. The myriad of amazing experiences I have had helped me grow intellectually and spiritually. Many of the things I write about in this book, I have learned from Gururaj in conjunction with his individually prescribed meditation practices that are a huge part of my life. Even though Gururaj has left the body and has merged into Unity Consciousness, his teachings still live on through his worldwide organizations including the American Meditation Society americanmeditationsociety.org, the British Meditation Society, the Spanish Meditation Society, the Danish Meditation Society, the Belgian Meditation Society, the Irish Meditation Society, the Israeli Meditation Society, the Canadian Meditation Society, and UK Meditation. I am grateful that I found Gururaj early in my lifetime. I have benefited tremendously and could not have been successful in passing on his profound teachings at prisons and to individual aspirants without his profound teachings and his spiritual guidance. Most of all, throughout my lifetime, I have learned how to **Be Brave!**

Personal Note to the Inmates from Doreena:

My deepest gratitude goes to you; you have shared your stories and hearts with me. I honor the Divinity that is within each and every one of you. I believe in you. You guys are truly amazing and imbedded in my heart. The more I know you, the more I see your beautiful shining spirits expressing yourself in the present moment. Your past deeds do not define who you really are. The past is behind you for a reason. It's ok to start over and it's ok to ask for help. Healing begins when you have honest conversations with yourself and can see the Divinity within yourselves and everyone else. You are all manifestations of God. Keep up with your meditations and spiritual practices and align yourselves with Divinity. I appreciate you for all of the things you have taught me while sharing your hearts, thoughts, and beautiful spirits. You have truly enriched my life. I am grateful that our paths have crossed. Go forward with love and grace. You are worthy and Divine.

My advice is to make the best of whatever life circumstances and situations you find yourselves in. There is a learning experience that needs to be revealed. Although life can be challenging and filled with potholes, there is joy and bliss along the way. Stay in the present moment, focus on the positives and see the light behind the clouds. Seeking moderation and balance in life are worthy goals. With a little perseverance and lining up your energies, anything is possible!

Doreena

ACKNOWLEDGMENTS

Mary Ann Starus has decades long editing experience and has been a dear friend throughout my adulthood. I am very grateful for her expertise and her invaluable criticism when she saw things that did not appear in my consciousness or realm of experiences. She believed in me and offered emotional support when I needed it most.

Lauren (Vida) Branscome is an author of 10 books. As a long time meditator from the American Meditation Society and spiritual friend, she has been instrumental in providing me with her invaluable insights and ability to uplift me with her caring heart and wisdom. I am so very grateful for her support.

My sister, **Donna Campos,** has been an avid reader since early childhood. My love of reading came from her. Several years ago we formed a sister bookclub. I learned about historical fiction of strong women who were the backbones of their famous husbands like Albert Einstein, Winston Churchill, and Franklin D. Roosevelt. When I began writing this book and doubted myself, she was behind me like an invisible shield to provide me with confidence to go forward and never give up.

My spiritual friend **Pingala Napier** provided input after reviewing the book. Her unconditional love has been a Godsend when I was experiencing multiple life challenges. She never gave up on me and I never felt judged.

Madhu Braunger provided her expertise as an advanced meditation teacher. She was instrumental in sharing my vision of starting a Prison Meditation Program by participating in the prison Orientation. I am grateful for her support.

I would also like to acknowledge all of the other meditators (too many to mention) from the American Meditation Society as well as our sister organizations around the world who support this project. I honor each and every one of them.

REFERENCES

1   National Institute of Corrections, December 31, (2020) p. 1
2   U.S. Religious Landscape Study. (2014), Pew Research Center, Washington, D.C. p. 23
3   Herculano-Houzel, S. (2009). The Human Brain in Numbers: A Linearly Scaled-up Primate Brain. Published online. 2009 Aug. 5. p. 33
4   Lozoff, S., Rubin, H. (2017). *We're all doing time.* Sheridan Books, Ann Arbor, MI. p. 41
5   Byrne, Rhonda. (2006). *The Secret.* Atria Books, Beyond Words Publishing. Australia. p. 56
6   Jefferson, W. (2009). *Reincarnation Beliefs of North American Indians.* Native Voices. p. 66
7   J. (1st Ed.) (2004) *Christian Meditation: Experiencing the Presence of God,* Harper Collins Publishers. p. 71
8   Benson, H. *Relaxation Response.* (2000). William Morrow Paperbacks. p. 92
9   Jackson, P., Delehanty, H. (1995). *Sacred Hoops: Spiritual Lessons of a Hardwood Warrior.* Hyperion, New York, New York. p. 150
10 Federal Bureau of Prisons www.bop.gov p. 182
11 Reuters: Health News, Oct. 12, 2016. p. 182
12 National Crime Victimization Study (2007), Department of Justice. p. 182
13 *The Four Agreements: A Toltec Wisdom Book* by Don Miguel Ruiz. p. 183

IMAGE CREDITS

The AMS symbol has a copyright, and cannot be reproduced without permission. As depicted in the symbol, the candle flame is surrounded by the major world religions and represents our own inner light. The golden cord means we are all connected no matter what religion we follow. The nine major religions are depicted below and the eternal circle encompasses all other religions.

Photographer:
Greg Weatherly

Photo Editor:
Gordon Hume

AFTERWORD

This book reveals Doreena's heartfelt desire to help others as you will see expressed through her story and experiences in the "Prison Meditation Program." What unfolds through her writing is the beautiful freedom that is liberated through the teaching of meditation that brings more light, balance, and love to our lives. She brings both the meditation practices and teachings of her spiritual teacher, carrying the torch of light as the "Bridge" to awaken and be more aware of the belief systems, conditioning, and programming that no longer serves us in a life supporting way. Life changing at best!

Lauren (Vida) Branscome, Author

Whether you're behind the razor wire or searching for insight on how to make a difference reversing the trends in the criminal justice system, this book is compelling and inspiring. Doreena lays out such clear, attainable instruction. Her personal narrative of a volunteer's journey into the prison system is authentic and gripping. It's bound to be a go-to resource for muting the monkey mind and taming the ego. The incarcerated community has such an experienced teacher and devoted advocate in Doreena Durbin. Don't pass up this read. She has unequivocal street cred to lead you to get an inner life!

Douglas O'Leary, released

GET AN INNER LIFE: MEDITATE Doreena Durbin, M.Ed
Contact: doreena1122@gmail.com

Printed in the United States
by Baker & Taylor Publisher Services